T0302700

Sew Cute & Clever

FARM & FOREST FRIENDS

Mix & Match 16 Paper-Pieced Blocks, 6 Home Decor Projects

Mary Hertel

C&T PUBLISHING

Publisher: Amy Marson

Creative Director: Gailen Runge

Acquisitions Editor: Roxane Cerda

Managing Editor: Liz Aneloski

Editor: Katie Van Amburg

Technical Editor: Linda Johnson

Cover/Book Designer: April Mostek

Production Coordinator: Tim Manibusan

Production Editor: Alice Mace Nakanishi

Illustrator: Aliza Shalit

Photo Assistants: Rachel Holmes and Mai Yong Vang

Style photography by Kelly Burgoyne, subjects photography by Mai Yong Vang, and instructional photography by Michael Gardner of C&T Publishing, Inc., unless otherwise noted

Published by C&T Publishing, Inc., P.O. Box 1456, Lafayette, CA 94549

Attention Teachers: C&T Publishing, Inc., encourages you to use this book as a text for teaching. Contact us at 800-284-1114 or ctpub.com for lesson plans and information about the C&T Creative Troupe.

Library of Congress Cataloging-in-Publication Data

Names: Hertel, Mary, 1955- author.

Title: Sew cute & clever farm & forest friends : mix & match 16 paper-pieced blocks, 6 home decor projects / Mary Hertel.

Other titles: Sew cute and clever farm and forest friends

Description: Lafayette : C&T Publishing, [2019]

Identifiers: LCCN 2018030784 | ISBN 9781617457777 (softcover)

Subjects: LCSH: Patchwork--Patterns. | Quilting--Patterns. | Patchwork quilts | Animals in art.

Classification: LCC TT835 .H4469 2019 | DDC 746.46/041--dc23

LC record available at https://lccn.loc.gov/2018030784

Printed in China

10 9 8 7 6 5 4 3 2 1

Dedication

I dedicate this book to my six siblings: my sisters, Vivian and Sharon, and my brothers, Jim, Kevin, Tom, and Doug. They inspire me with their unique creativeness. Their support means a lot to me.

Acknowledgments

Thank you to my special friend Tom Warstler. His wisdom, patience, and support is always appreciated.

Contents

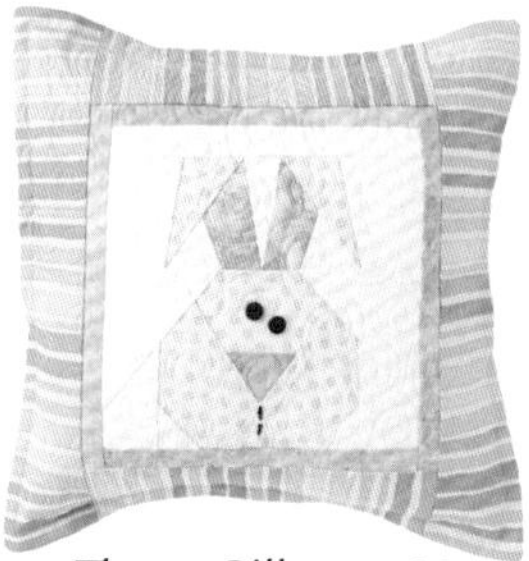

INTRODUCTION

Are you afraid to try paper piecing? Have you tried it in the past and been overwhelmed by too many tiny pieces? I suggest this: Try one of my patterns. As a designer, I promise to create the easiest paper-pieced blocks: blocks that assemble quickly, but are still as cute as can be.

Paper piecing is a very pure method of sewing an image into a quilt, yet it allows more flexibility than regular piecing. Unlike appliqué, the paper-pieced image is actually sewn into your project. Don't get me wrong, I respect appliqué and piecing, but the "puzzle-like" quality of putting together a paper pieced design has me hooked ... and I'd love to get you hooked, too!

I like to call it "sew by number." Just follow the numbers and add each scrap of fabric in numerical order. If you can count, you can paper piece! All the seams are straight lines, so it couldn't be easier.

This book is devoted to animal blocks. What is it about animals that make them so endearing? Having grown up on a dairy farm in central Wisconsin, I was surrounded by animals. Farm, woodland, domestic, or wild ... I loved them all. Animals are my favorite design topic, and also the favorite of my customers. My goal is to give each animal an expression all their own. The more expressive the animal, the better.

Now for the best part ... all sixteen paper-pieced blocks in this book work in any of the six different projects. And that's not all. The paper-pieced blocks in *any* of my books work for all my projects. That's right: all blocks are completely interchangeable in any of my books. Mix and match blocks and projects between my books as you like. This allows you to be truly creative!

So, please give it a try! Follow the simple step-by-step directions and open up to my world ... the world of paper piecing.

PAPER-PIECING BASICS

Paper piecing is a simple, straightforward method of sewing a design into a project. Perhaps you have experienced the joy and satisfaction of seeing the finished image after adding the last piece to a jigsaw puzzle. The effects of paper piecing are no different. Anyone with basic sewing skills can master paper piecing, as the approach used in this book is essentially sewing by number. Paper piecing is also a creative means of using up oddly shaped pieces of fabric that might otherwise have been relegated to the scrap pile.

Tools

- Paper (I recommend Carol Doak's Foundation Paper by C&T Publishing.)
- Sharp scissors
- Rotary cutter and mat
- Ruler with an easy-to-read ¼″ line (such as Add-A-Quarter ruler by CM Designs)
- Multiuse tool (such as Alex Anderson's 4-in-1 Essential Sewing Tool by C&T Publishing) or seam ripper
- Flat-head straight pins
- Lamp or natural light source
- Sewing machine
- Iron and pressing board

Things to Know

STITCH LENGTH

Set the stitch length at 1.5, which is about 20 stitches per inch. When paper piecing, the stitch perforations must be close together to allow the paper to rip easily, but not so close that ripping out a seam is an impossible task.

PREPARE A CONVENIENT WORK STATION

Have the iron, pressing board, and cutting mat close to the sewing machine. There should be a light source handy for positioning scrap pieces on the back of the block. A window works well during the day and a lamp at night.

THE BUTTERFLY EFFECT

After sewing a seamline, the fabric is flipped behind the numbered piece that you are currently attaching. This creates a butterfly effect, meaning that the fabric scrap needs to be lined up to the seam in such a way that it will cover the space you are sewing after it is flipped into place. If you are concerned that the size of the scrap is insufficient, pin along the seamline and try flipping the scrap into place before sewing the seam. If the scrap does not cover the area sufficiently, you can adjust it or find a larger scrap.

FOLLOW ALONG

If you are new to paper piecing, practice with the Raccoon block (page 45) as you read the following instructions.

Preparing the Patterns

1. Make the recommended number of color copies of the original block. (You need 2 copies for the Raccoon block.)

2. Cut the block into the segments denoted by the capital letters, *adding ¼″ seam allowances along the red lines and the outside edges of the block.* For the example, use 1 copy for each of the Segments A and B.

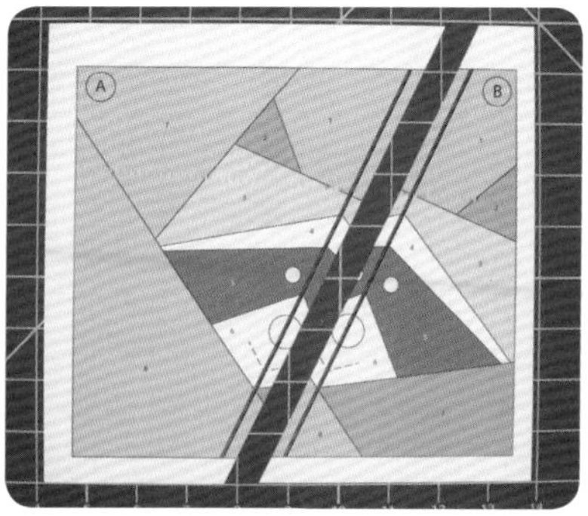

Segments A and B with ¼″ seam allowances all around

Paper Piecing a Segment

Always stitch pieces in numerical order. Don't forget to set the stitch length (page 7) to 1.5, or about 20 stitches per inch.

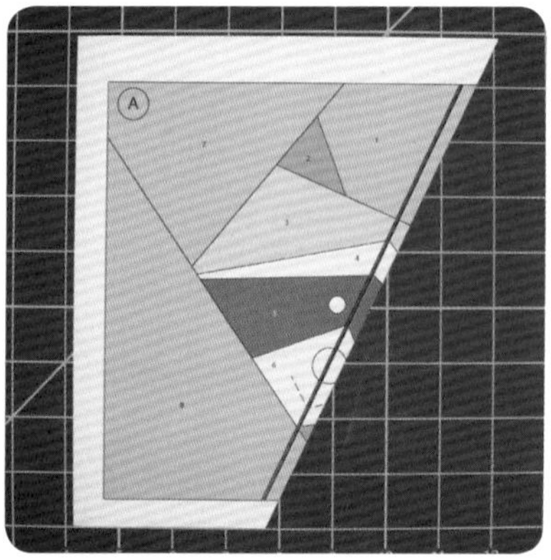

Front side of Segment A

1. Pin the *wrong* side of the Piece 1 fabric onto the *unprinted* side of the paper pattern. The right side of the fabric faces you (away from the paper).

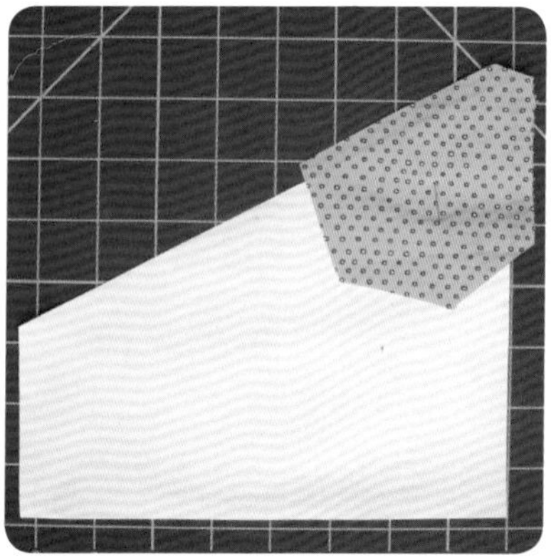

2. Bend the paper pattern and fabric along the seamline between Pieces 1 and 2. Use the side of a pencil or pressing tool (such as the presser cap on Alex Anderson's 4-in-1 Essential Sewing Tool) to put a nice crease in the fabric. (This will help you align the fabric for Piece 2.)

3. Align the Piece 2 fabric with the Piece 1 fabric by bending the paper along the seamline between Pieces 1 and 2 with the fabrics right sides together. The fabric for Piece 2 will be flipped into place after sewing. Use a generous ½″ seam allowance (this seam will be trimmed later). Pin in place, right sides together.

Tip: Right Sides Together

As you piece, always place the fabrics right sides together.

4 Sew ¼″ beyond the seamline at the beginning and the end of this seam (as shown by the green line). No backtacking is needed, as the ends of the seams are stitched over by other seams. Notice that the fabric for Piece 2 is much larger than needed; it will be trimmed later.

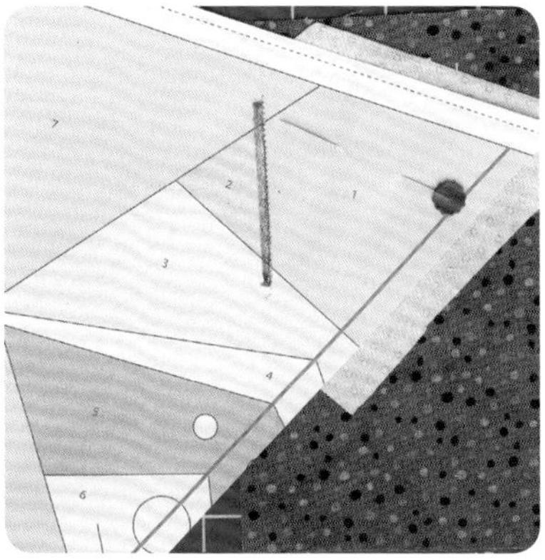

5 Fold the paper pattern out of the way along the stitching line and trim the seam allowance to ¼″, using scissors or a rotary cutter, mat, and ¼″ ruler.

6 Flip the fabric into position behind Piece 2 and press. The fabric needs to be trimmed on 2 other sides of Piece 2. Trim the fabric a generous ½″ beyond the first edge of Piece 2.

Tip: Double-Check to Avoid Seam Ripping

I like to use large scraps (but no larger than 9″ × 11″) and trim the piece after sewing it in place. As you place the fabric under the presser foot to sew, the seam allowance and the shape you are filling should be to your right. The shape you previously completed should be to your left. Before sewing, do a mental check. Ask yourself these two questions: "Is the piece I am working on to my right?" and "Is the majority of my fabric to my left?" If the answer is yes, then sew. This simple check will eliminate much seam ripping.

7 Lift the pattern away from the edge of Piece 2 so that it is out of the way. *Do not cut the pattern.* Trim the fabric a generous ½″ beyond the second edge of Piece 2.

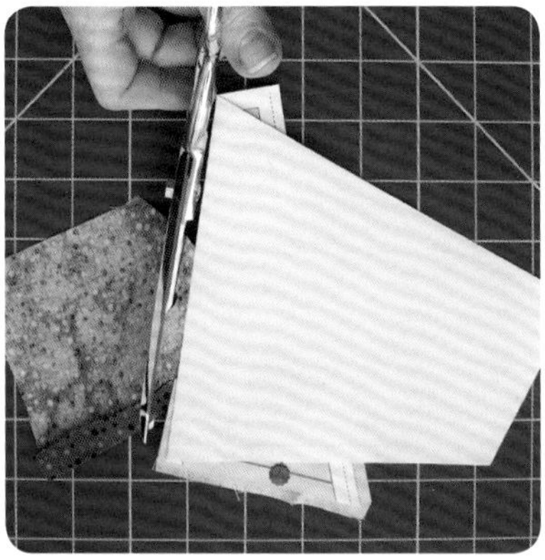

8 Continue to add the remaining pieces in the same manner as you added Piece 2.

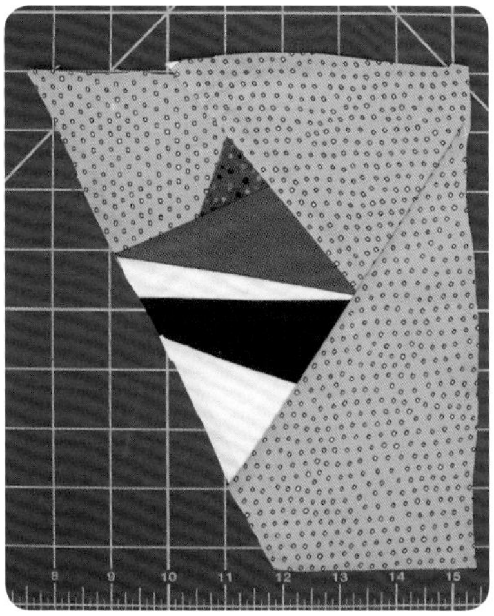

Segment A completed

Tip: Stitches Interfering?

Overstitching the seams may at times interfere with an exact fold along a stitching line. In this case, tear the paper just enough to release it from the stitching.

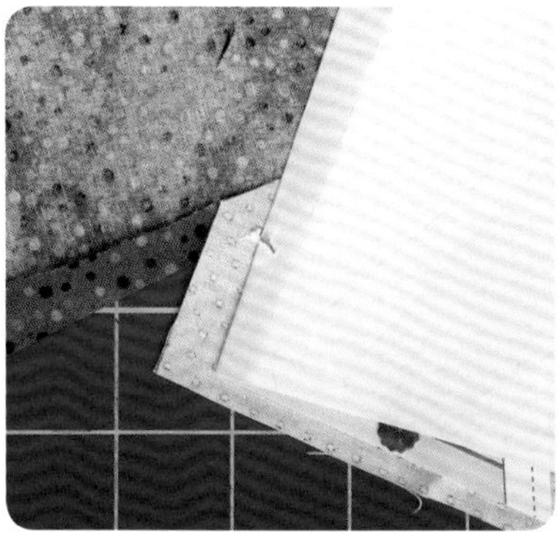

Tip: Remembering the Sequence

Use the word "STOP" to remember the sequence of steps:

- S = *Stitch*
- T = *Trim*
- O = *Open*
- P = *Press*

9 Trim the seam allowance of the segment to an *exact* ¼″ seam, using a rotary cutter, a mat, and a ruler with a ¼″ line.

The segment is now ready to be sewn to the other segments. Follow the same process to make Segment B.

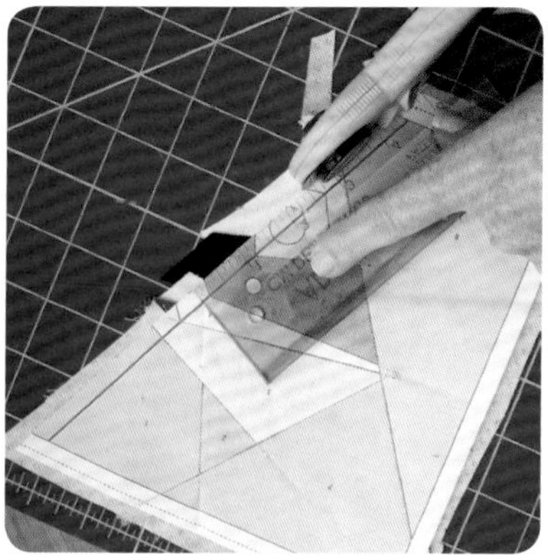

Joining Segments

Note: Make sure each segment is trimmed so that it has an exact ¼″ seam allowance along the segment seamline. Do not trim the outer edge seam allowances at this time.

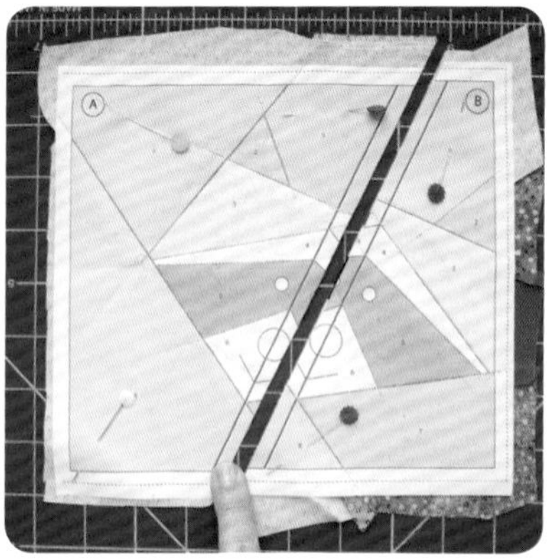

Segments have ¼″ seam allowances where they will be joined.

1 With right sides together, pin the edges of Segments A and B, matching the red sewing lines. Push a straight pin through the end of each red line to help align them as closely as possible. Sew on the center black line and ¼″ past the red line on both ends.

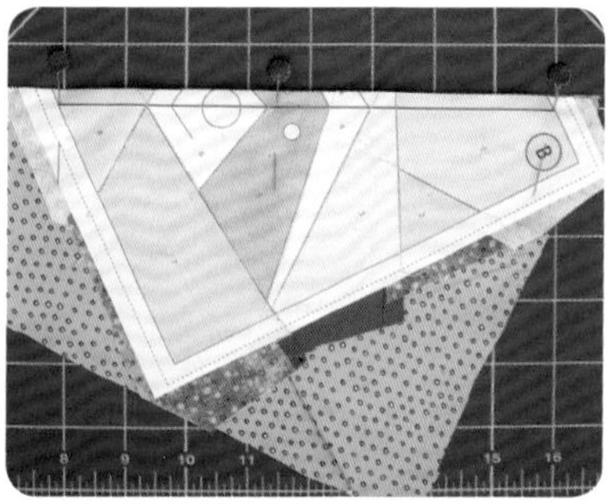

Sew segments together on center black line.

2 Remove the paper from the seam allowance to eliminate the possibility of the paper getting trapped under the seams.

3 Press the seam to a side. Let the seam "show" you in which direction it wants to be pressed.

4 When you have completed the block, square it to the dimensions indicated on the pattern. If the block pattern finishes at 7½″ square, trim the block to 8″ square to allow for ¼″ seam allowances.

Tip: Finish before Trimming

Make sure never to trim the excess fabric from the outer edges of the block until the block is finished.

5 Complete any embroidery and add any sashing before removing the paper. The paper acts as a stabilizer and keeps the block from stretching. After the block has been attached to the project, the paper may be removed.

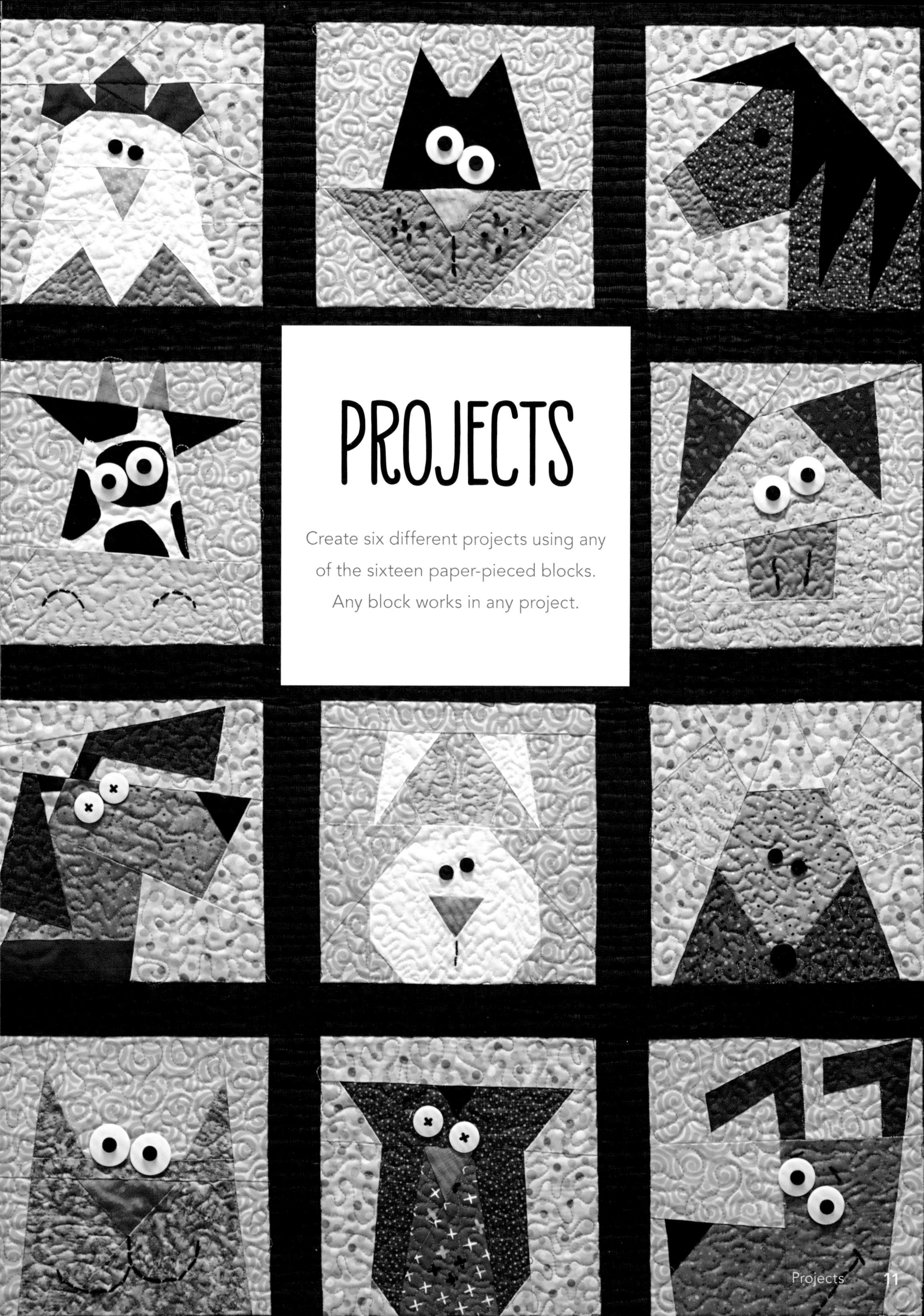

PROJECTS

Create six different projects using any of the sixteen paper-pieced blocks. Any block works in any project.

QUILT

FINISHED SIZE: 38½″ × 47½″

Cuddle up with a good book and this lap-size quilt adorned with your favorite animals.

MATERIALS

Fabric requirements are based on 40″-wide fabric.

Fabric A: ⅝ yard for sashing

Fabric B: ¾ yard for border

Fabric C: ½ yard for binding

Fabric D: 1½ yards for backing

Fabric E: 1½ yards total background fabric for paper-pieced blocks

Assorted scraps: To paper piece 12 blocks

Batting: 44″ × 53″

Assorted buttons

Black embroidery floss

CUTTING

WOF = width of fabric. Fold fabric selvage to selvage.

Fabric A

- Cut 9 strips 2″ × WOF. Subcut 2 strips into 2″ × 8″ rectangles for a total of 8 sashing strips.

Fabric B

- Cut 4 strips 5½″ × WOF for border.

Fabric C

- Cut 5 strips 2½″ × WOF for binding.

Sewing

Use ¼″ seams throughout, unless otherwise directed.

PAPER-PIECED BLOCKS

Refer to Paper-Piecing Basics (page 7) as needed.
Refer to Block Patterns (pages 37–53) to choose blocks.

1. Paper piece 12 selected blocks, using Fabric E as the background fabric of each block and the assorted scraps for the rest of the block. You'll notice, I used 2 different fabrics for E and made half the animals with one background and the rest with the other background.

2. Add any necessary embroidery to the blocks. Do not add any buttons at this time, but mark their placement. If this quilt will be used for a baby, appliqué fabric circles for the eyes instead of using buttons, which might be a choking hazard.

3. Trim each block to 8″ × 8″.

ADD THE SASHING

1. With right sides together, sew a Fabric A sashing strip 2″ × 8″ to the right side of a paper-pieced block. Repeat this process with a second paper-pieced block.

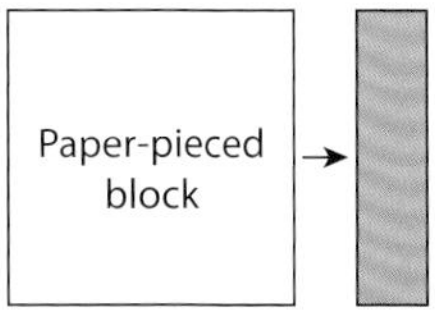

2. Sew the 2 blocks together.

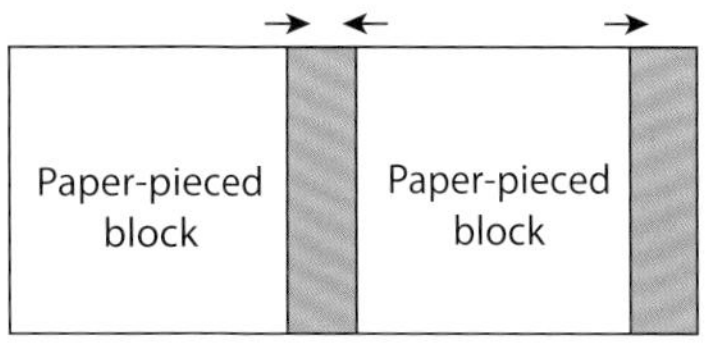

3 Sew a third paper-pieced block to the end of the row. Press the seams away from the blocks. (See pressing arrows.)

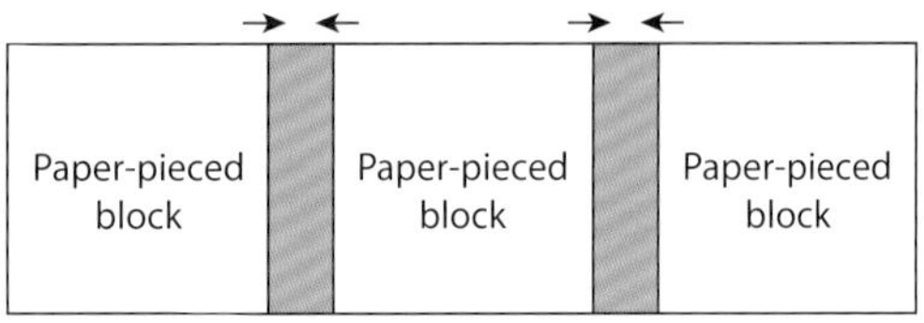

Row 1

4 Repeat Steps 1–3 to make 3 more rows in this manner. There are 4 horizontal rows with 3 blocks in each row.

5 Sew a Fabric A WOF sashing strip to the top of each row and the bottom of the last row of blocks. Trim any excess from the ends of the strips with a rotary cutter and ruler. Join all the rows. Press the seams away from the blocks.

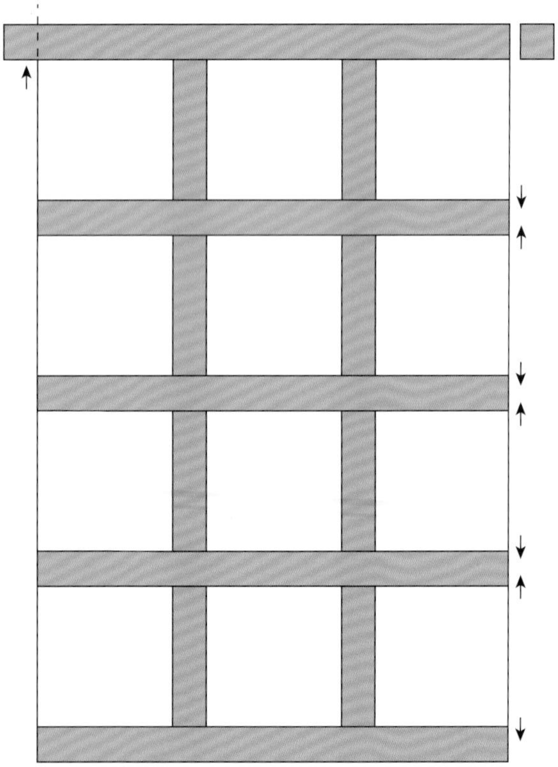

Trim excess from each strip.

6 Sew the remaining Fabric A WOF strips to the vertical sides of the quilt. Trim the excess strips. Press the seams away from the blocks.

ADD THE BORDER

1 Sew a Fabric B border strip to the sides of the quilt. Trim any excess from the sides of the strips.

2 Sew another Fabric B border strip to the top and bottom of the quilt. Trim any excess from the sides of the strips.

QUILTING

1 Remove the paper from the back of the blocks.

2 Layer the quilt (right side facing up), batting, and backing (right side facing down).

3 Pin together all 3 layers, and quilt as desired.

4 Trim the excess backing and batting, squaring up the quilt.

BINDING

1 Pin 2 Fabric C binding strips together, overlapping on a right (90°) angle, with right sides together. Mark a diagonal line from Corner A to Corner B. Sew on the diagonal line to connect the strips. Trim the seam to ¼″ and press to one side. Continue, adding the rest of the 4 strips together in this manner to make 1 long, continuous strip.

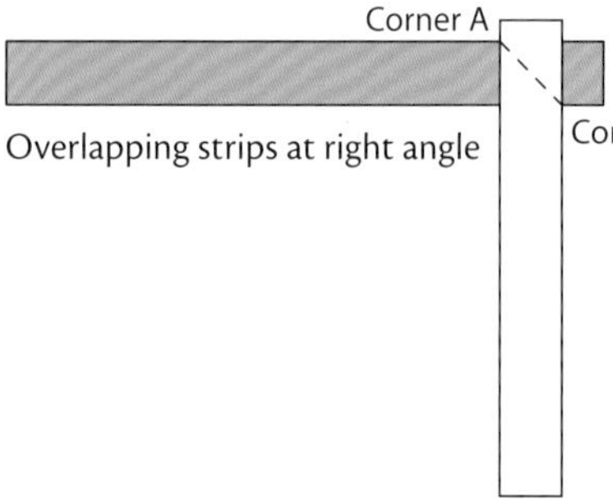

Overlapping strips at right angle

2 Press the WOF strips in half lengthwise, with wrong sides together.

3 Align the raw edges of the binding strip with the raw edges of the quilt. Fold the beginning of the strip on a right angle, with the tail facing away from the quilt.

4 Stitch ¼″ from the raw edges. Stop stitching ¼″ from the first corner. Backtack.

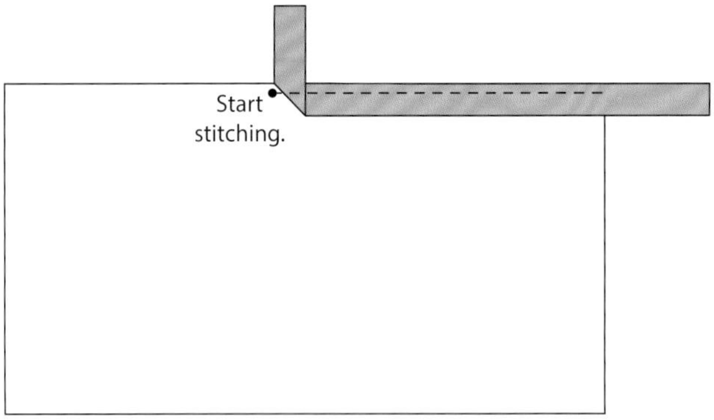

Binding start

5 Fold the binding strip straight up. The raw edge of the binding strip should align with the raw edge of the second side of the quilt.

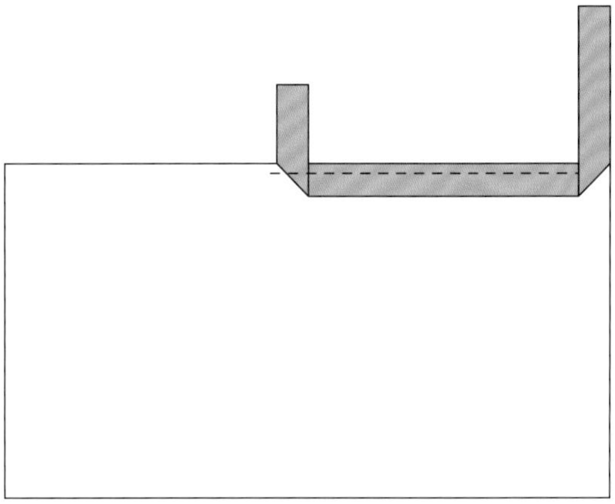
Starting first corner

6 Fold the binding strip straight down to overlap the second edge of the quilt. Start stitching at the top corner and continue until ¼″ from the next corner. Backtack.

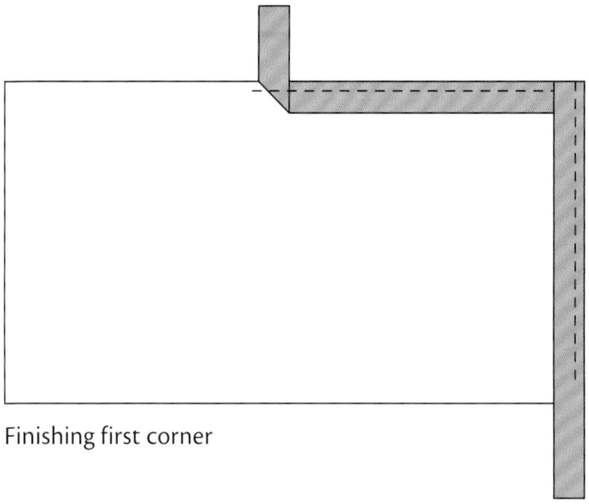
Finishing first corner

7 Continue in this manner around the remaining sides of the quilt, backtacking and turning at each corner.

8 Trim the end of the binding strip so it overlaps the angled beginning section by 2″. Trim away the beginning tail.

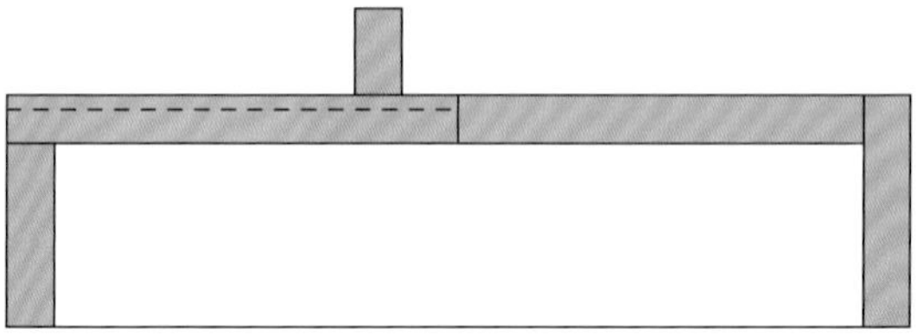
Overlap binding tails.

9 Press the binding around to the back of the quilt, and hand stitch in place, easing in the fullness where the tails overlap.

FINISHING

Hand sew any necessary buttons to the paper-pieced blocks, sewing through all thicknesses.

TABLE TOPPER

FINISHED SIZE: 23″ diameter

Wouldn't this table topper be charming at a rustic cabin?

MATERIALS

Fabric requirements are based on 40″-wide fabric.

Fabric A: ½ yard background fabric for paper-pieced blocks

Fabric B: ½ yard for main fabric and binding

Fabric C: ¾ yard for backing

Assorted scraps: To paper piece 4 blocks

Batting: 27″ × 27″ square

Assorted buttons

Black embroidery floss

CUTTING

WOF = width of fabric. Fold fabric selvage to selvage.

Fabric B

- Cut 2 squares 8⅜″ × 8⅜″. Subcut on the diagonal for a total of 4 side triangles.
- Cut 1 square 8″ × 8″ for center square.
- Cut 2 strips 2½″ × WOF for binding.

Sewing

Use ¼″ seams throughout, unless otherwise directed.

PAPER-PIECED BLOCKS

Refer to Paper-Piecing Basics (page 7) as needed.

Refer to Block Patterns (pages 37–53) to choose blocks.

1. Paper piece 4 selected blocks, using Fabric A for the background fabric of each block and the assorted scraps for the rest of the block.

2. Add any necessary embroidery to the blocks. Do not add any buttons at this time, but mark their placement. If this will be used as a baby play mat, appliqué fabric circles for the eyes instead of using buttons, which might be a choking hazard.

3. Trim each block to 8″ × 8″.

CONSTRUCT THE ROWS

Tip: Block Placement

The orientation of the blocks in this project is up to you. I wrote the instructions so that the table topper is interesting from all directions, but you can adjust the placement direction as desired.

1. Sew the 8⅜″ edge of a Fabric B side triangle to each side of a paper-pieced block to make Row 1. Make sure the right angle (90°) corner of the triangle aligns with the top corner of the block. Press the seams away from the blocks. Repeat this process to make Row 3.

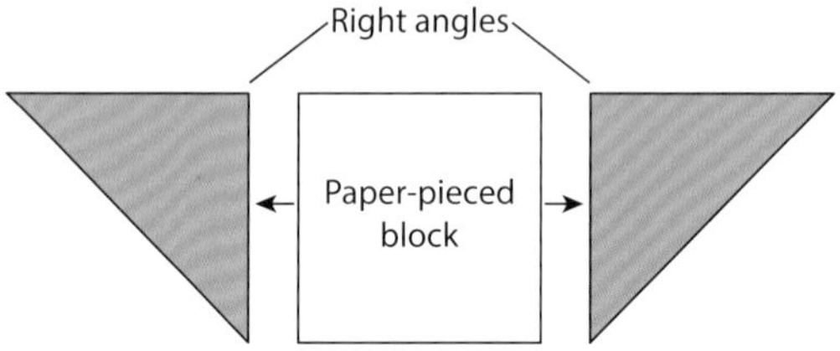

Rows 1 and 3: Right angle corners aligned with top of block

2. Sew 2 paper-pieced blocks to either side of the Fabric B center square to make Row 2. Press the seams away from the block.

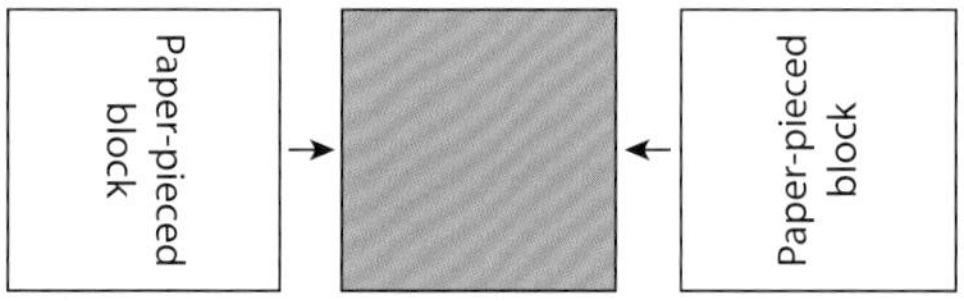

Row 2: Place paper-pieced blocks sideways.

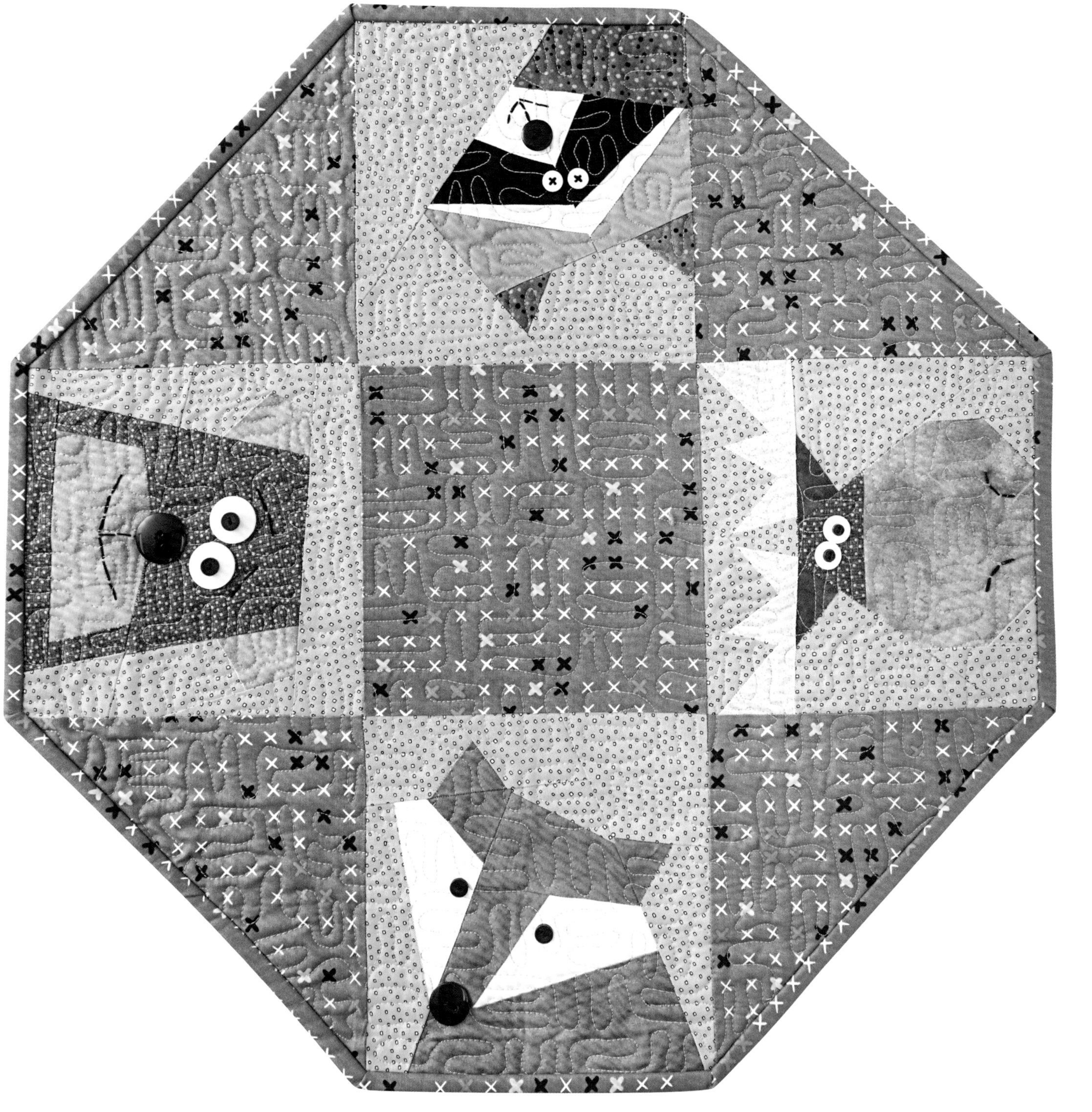

ATTACH THE ROWS

1 Sew the bottom of Row 1 to the top of Row 2, matching the seamlines.

2 Sew the bottom of Row 2 to the top of Row 3, matching the seamlines. Press the seams to one side.

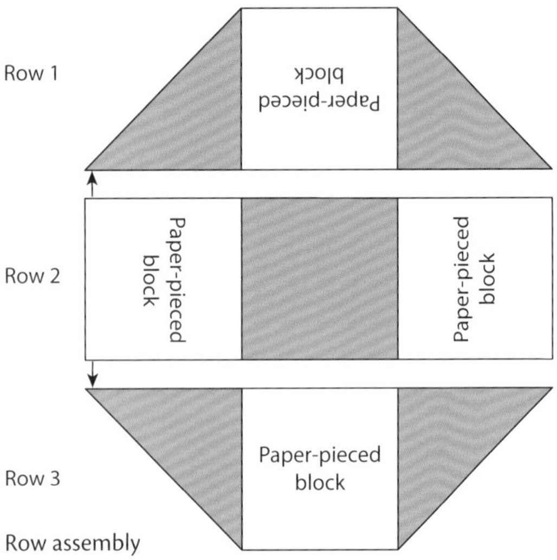

Row assembly

QUILTING

1 Remove the paper from the back of the blocks.

2 Layer the table topper (right side facing up), batting, and backing (right side facing down).

3 Pin together all 3 layers, and quilt as desired.

4 Trim the excess batting and backing, straightening up the sides of the table topper.

BINDING

1 Overlap the 2 Fabric B binding strips on a right angle (90°), with right sides together. Mark a diagonal line from Corner A to Corner B. Sew on the diagonal line. Trim the seams to ¼″ and press to one side.

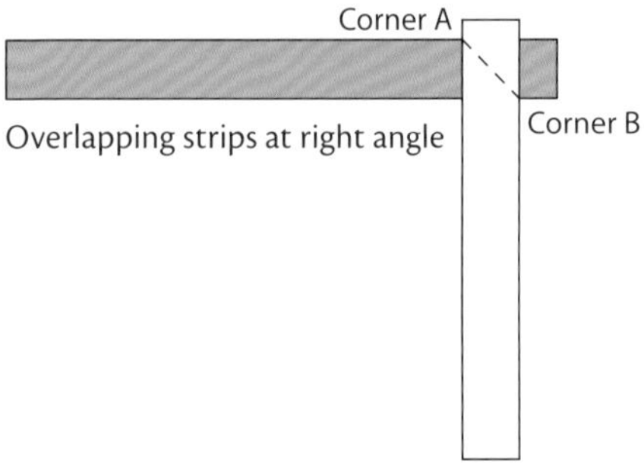

Overlapping strips at right angle

2 Press the strips in half lengthwise, with wrong sides together.

3 Fold the beginning of the binding strip on a right angle with the tail facing away from the table topper.

4 Stitch ¼″ from the raw edges. Stop stitching ¼″ from the first corner. Backtack.

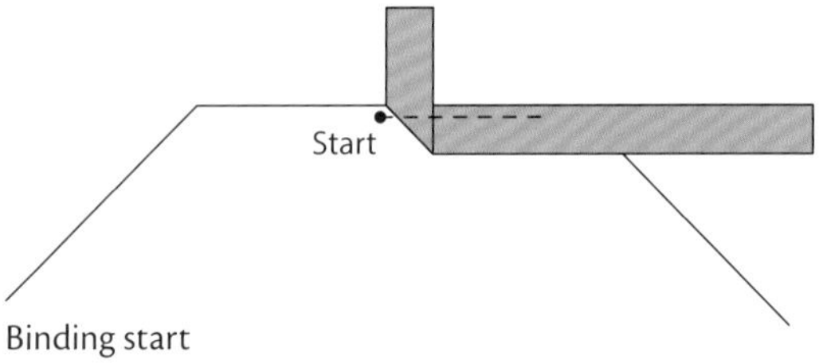

Binding start

5 Fold the binding strip up. The strip will point up at a bit of an angle, as shown.

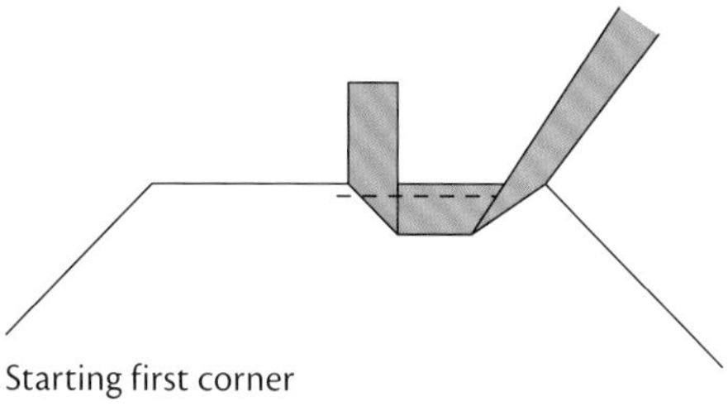

Starting first corner

6 Fold the binding strip down to overlap the second edge of the table topper. Start stitching at the top corner and continue until ¼″ from the next corner. Backtack.

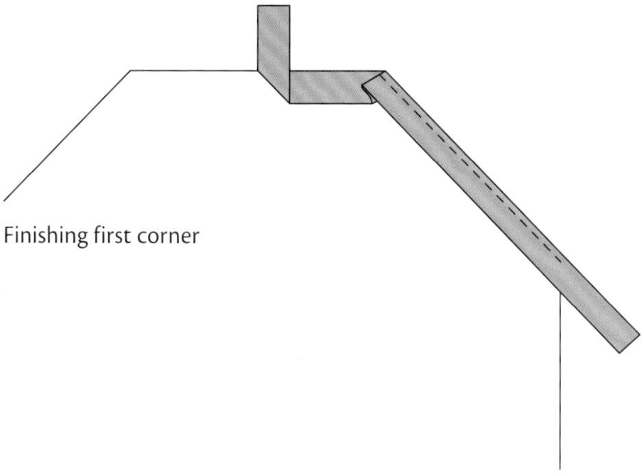

Finishing first corner

7 Continue in this manner around the remaining sides of the table topper, backtacking and turning at each corner.

8 Overlap the tail of the binding about 2″ past the right-angled section at the beginning of the binding. Trim the remainder of the binding strip and the beginning of the tail.

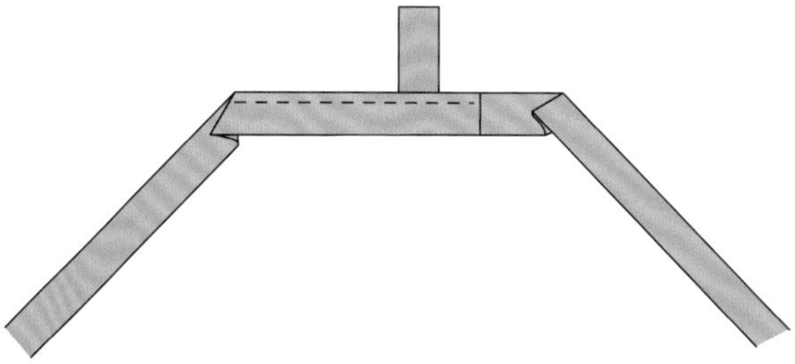

Overlapping binding

9 Trim the excess backing and batting.

10 Press the binding around to the back of the table topper, and hand stitch in place, easing in the fullness where the tails overlap.

FINISHING

Hand sew any necessary buttons to the paper-pieced blocks, sewing through all thicknesses.

Table Runner / Bench Pillow

FINISHED TABLE RUNNER: 17½″ × 39½″
FINISHED BENCH PILLOW: 17½″ × 39½″ × 6″

Whether as a runner or pillow, this sweet design is great for adding color to a table, bench, or sofa.

Note: *Follow the materials list, cutting list, and initial sewing instructions below for both projects. If you are making the table runner, continue with the instructions in Table Runner Details (page 25). If you are making the bench pillow, skip ahead to the instructions in Bench Pillow Details (page 26).*

Materials

The fabrics and cutting for the table runner and the bench pillow are the same unless otherwise noted. Fabric requirements are based on 40″-wide fabric.

Fabric A: ⅓ yard background fabric for paper-pieced blocks

Fabric B: ¼ yard for inner border

Fabric C:

For table runner: 1¾ yards for outer border and backing

For bench pillow: 1⅛ yards for outer border and back

Fabric D: *For bench pillow only:* ⅝ yard for lining (muslin works well)

Fabric E: *For table runner only:* ⅓ yard for binding

Assorted scraps: To paper piece 3 blocks

Batting: 25″ × 50″ piece

Pillow form: *For bench pillow only:* 16″ × 38″

Hook-and-loop tape: *For bench pillow only:* 12″ long

Assorted buttons

Black embroidery floss

Cutting

Fold fabric selvage to selvage for WOF (width of fabric) cuts, unless otherwise directed.

Fabric B

- Cut 3 strips 2″ × WOF. Subcut 1 strip into 4 sashing strips 2″ × 8″.

Fabric C

For outer borders:

- Cut 2 strips 4″ × WOF.
- Cut 1 strip 6″ × WOF. Subcut into 2 rectangles 6″ × 11″.

For bench pillow back:

Open fabric flat.

- Cut 2 rectangles 17½″ × 24″.

For table runner back:

Open fabric flat.

- Cut 1 rectangle 23″ × 45″.

Fabric D (*bench pillow only*)

Open fabric flat.

- Cut 1 rectangle 18″ × 40″.

Fabric E (*table runner only*)

- Cut 3 strips 2½″ × WOF for binding.

Batting

For bench pillow:

- Cut 1 rectangle 18″ × 40″.

For table runner:

- Cut 1 rectangle 23″ × 45″.

Sewing

Use ¼″ seams throughout, unless otherwise directed. The sewing instructions for the table topper and the bench pillow are the same unless otherwise noted.

PAPER-PIECED BLOCKS

Refer to Paper-Piecing Basics (page 7) as needed.

Refer to Block Patterns (pages 37–53) to choose blocks.

1. Paper piece 3 selected blocks, using Fabric A for the background fabric of each block and the assorted scraps for the rest of the block.

2. Add any necessary embroidery to the blocks. Do not add any buttons at this time, but mark their placement. If this project will be used for a baby, appliqué fabric circles for the eyes instead of using buttons, which might be a choking hazard.

3. Trim each block to 8″ × 8″.

ADD THE SASHING

1. With right sides together, sew a Fabric B sashing strip 2″ × 8″ to the left side of a paper-pieced block. Press seams away from the block.

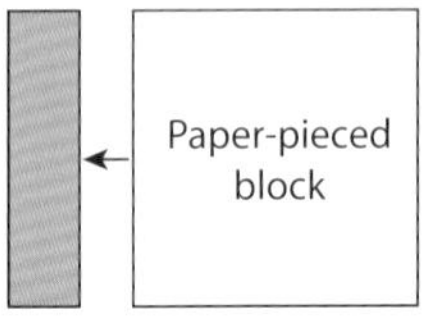

2. Repeat Step 1 with the remaining 2 paper-pieced blocks.

3. Sew the 3 blocks together to create a row.

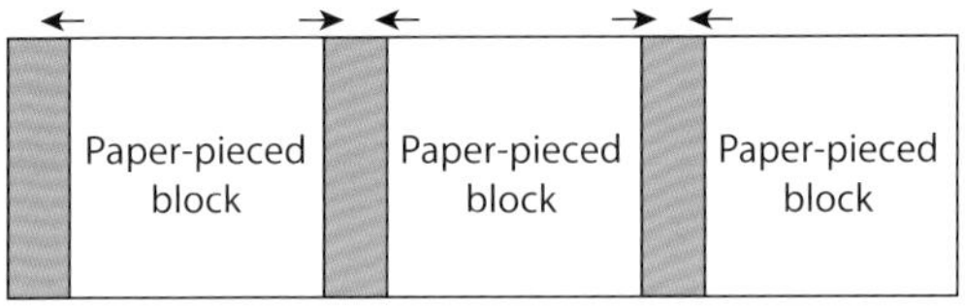

3 blocks sewn together

4. Sew the remaining Fabric B sashing strip to the far right end of the row.

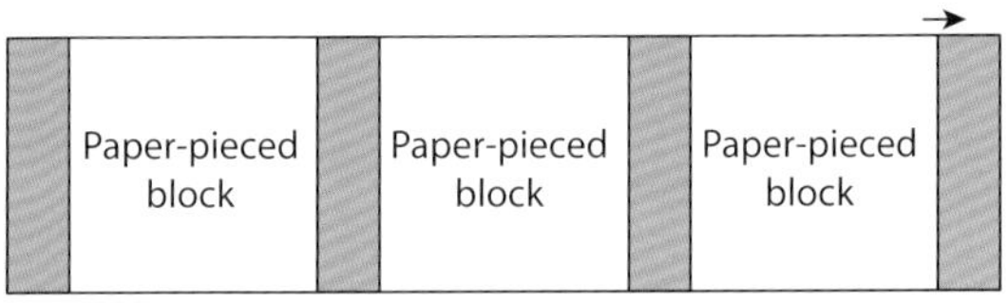

Row of blocks with sashing

5. Sew the 2 Fabric B 2″ strips to the top and bottom of the row.

6. Trim away any excess from the WOF strips.

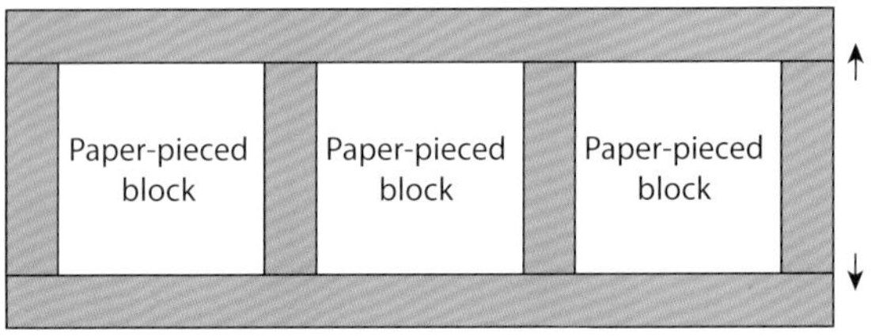

Completed row

ADD THE BORDER

1. With right sides together, sew the Fabric C rectangles 6″ × 11″ to each side edge of the unit.

2. With right sides together, sew the 2 Fabric C 4″ strips to the top and bottom of the unit.

3. Trim away any excess fabric strip with a rotary cutter and ruler. Press the seams towards the borders.

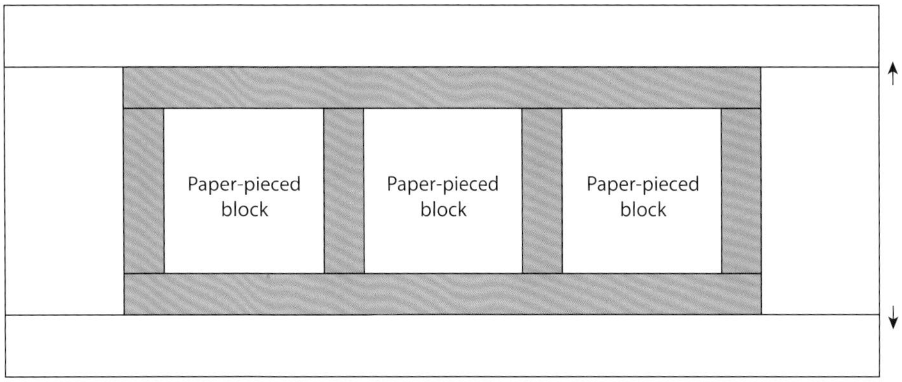

Trimmed, completed front

NOTE: *If you are making the table runner, continue with the instructions in Table Runner Details (below). If you are making the bench pillow, skip ahead to the instructions in Bench Pillow Details (page 26).*

TABLE RUNNER DETAILS

For materials, cutting, and initial sewing instructions, see Table Runner / Bench Pillow (pages 22–25). Then use the following instructions to complete the table runner.

QUILTING

1. Remove the paper from the back of the blocks.

2. Layer the table runner (right side facing up), batting, and backing (right side facing down).

3. Pin together all 3 layers, and quilt as desired.

4. Trim the excess batting and backing, squaring up the table runner.

BINDING

Follow the instructions for the quilt binding (see Binding, page 14), using the Fabric E binding strips.

FINISHING

Hand sew any necessary buttons to the paper-pieced blocks, sewing through all thicknesses.

Bench Pillow Details

For materials, cutting, and initial sewing instructions, see Table Runner / Bench Pillow (pages 22–25). Then use the following instructions to complete the bench pillow.

QUILTING

1 Remove the paper from the back of the blocks.

2 Layer the pillow front (right side facing up), batting, and 18″ × 40″ rectangle of lining (right side facing down). Pin or baste together. Quilt through all layers as desired.

3 Trim the pillow top to 17½″ × 39½″.

PREPARE THE PILLOW BACK

1 Press the raw edge under 1″ on a 17½″ side of each of the 2 Fabric C pillow backs. Press under another 1″ on the same 2 edges.

2 Topstitch the pressed edges to form a hem along one edge of each rectangle.

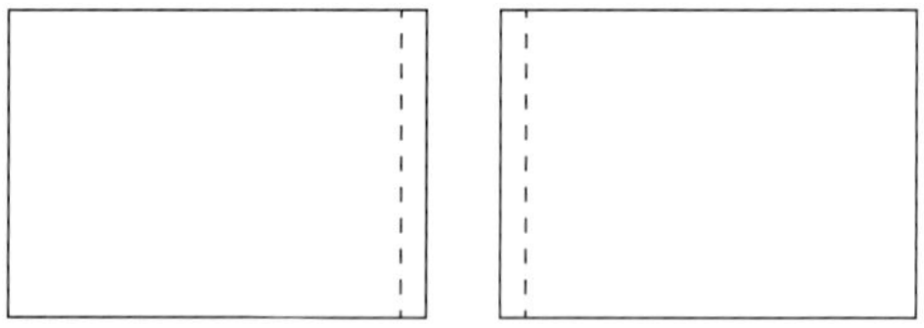

Both pillow backs hemmed on one side

3 With the right sides facing up, overlap the hemmed edges of the 2 rectangles. Slide the 12″ piece of hook-and-loop tape between the 2 hemmed edges. Pin the female section of the hook-and-loop tape to the back of the hemmed area on the top section. Pin the male section to the front of the hemmed area on the bottom section. This enables the female and male edges to join properly.

4 Sew around the edges of each hook-and-loop tape strip to secure them to the pillow back pieces.

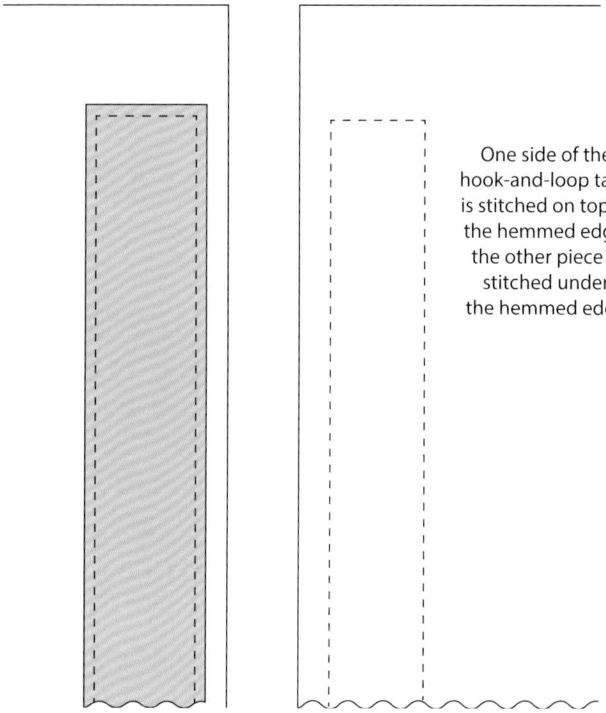

Hook-and-loop tape positioning

SEW THE PILLOW FRONT TO THE PILLOW BACK

1. Stick the female and male strips of hook-and-loop tape together. Lay the pillow back on a cutting mat, right side up.

2. Pin the pillow front to the pillow back, right sides together. *Note:* The pillow back is a bit generous in size. The hook-and-loop tape should be close to the center of the pillow back.

3. Trim away any excess from the pillow backs' side edges.

4. With a ¼″ seam allowance, sew all the way around the 4 sides of the pillow.

5. Remove the pins and turn the pillow right side out, through the hook-and-loop tape opening. Gently push out the corners. Press the edges flat.

6. Topstitch ½″ away from the edge of the pillow.

FINISHING

1. Hand sew any necessary buttons to the paper-pieced blocks, sewing through all thicknesses.

2. Slide the 16″ × 38″ pillow form through the back opening.

PILLOWCASE

FINISHED SIZE: 20½″ × 26″

Your loved ones will enjoy going to sleep with their favorite animals.

MATERIALS

Fabric requirements are based on 40″-wide fabric.

Fabric A: 1 yard for main color (*Note:* I have allowed for extra fabric, in case it is directional.)

Fabric B: ½ yard for cuff and sashing

Fabric C: ½ yard for lining (Muslin is recommended.)

Fabric D: ½ yard background fabric for paper-pieced blocks

Fusible fleece: ½ yard of 45″ wide or ¾ yard of 20″ wide

Assorted scraps: To paper piece 3 blocks

Assorted buttons

Black embroidery floss

CUTTING

Fold fabric selvage to selvage for WOF (width of fabric) cuts, unless otherwise directed.

Fabric A

Open fabric flat.

- Cut 1 rectangle 23″ × 25¼″ for pillowcase main fabric.
- Cut 1 rectangle 4″ × 23″ for bottom front.

Fabric B

- Cut 2 strips 1½″ × 23″ for sashing.
- Cut 1 rectangle 10″ × WOF for cuff.

Fabric C

Open fabric flat.

- Cut 1 rectangle 15″ × 23″ for lining.

Fabric D

Open fabric flat. Cut the background rectangle first. Use the remainder of the fabric to paper piece the blocks.

- Cut 1 rectangle 5″ × 23″ for background.

Fusible fleece

- Cut 1 rectangle 15″ × 23″.

Sewing

Use ¼″ seams throughout, unless otherwise directed.

PAPER-PIECED BLOCKS

Refer to Paper-Piecing Basics (page 7) as needed.
Refer to Block Patterns (pages 37–53) to choose blocks.

1. Paper piece 3 selected blocks, using Fabric D for the background fabric of each block and the assorted scraps for the rest of the block.

2. Add any necessary embroidery to the blocks. Do not add any buttons at this time, but mark their placement. If this pillowcase will be used for a baby, appliqué fabric circles for the eyes instead of using buttons, which might be a choking hazard.

3. Trim each block to 8″ × 8″.

ASSEMBLE THE BLOCKS

1. Sew the 3 paper-pieced blocks together along their side edges. Press the seams open.

2. Sew the Fabric D background rectangle to the top of the 3 blocks. Press the seams away from the blocks.

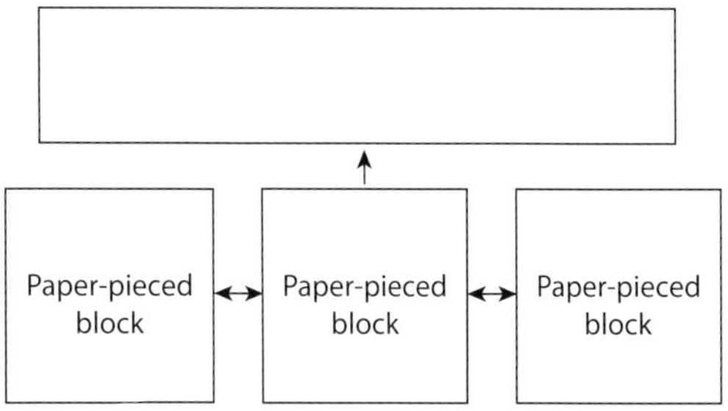

ADD THE SASHING

1. Sew a Fabric B 1½″ sashing strip to the top and bottom of the block unit.

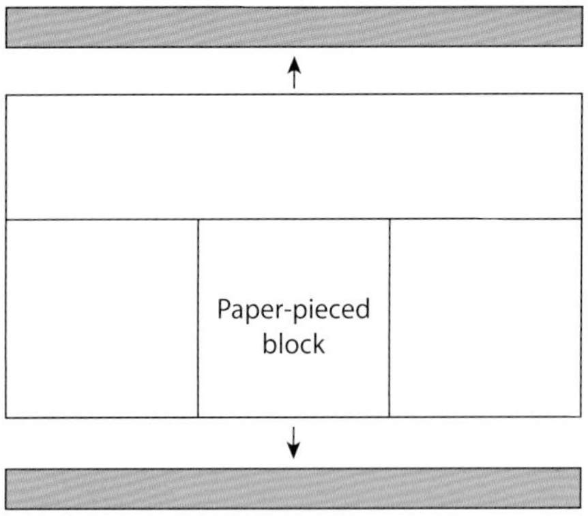

2. Press the seams toward the sashing.

QUILT THE BLOCK UNIT

1. Remove the paper from the back of the paper-pieced blocks.

2. Steam press the fusible fleece to the back of the block unit.

3. Quilt as desired.

4. Hand sew any necessary buttons to the paper-pieced blocks.

5. *Optional:* Satin stitch or machine embroider a name (or another word) in the background area above the 3 paper-pieced blocks.

PILLOWCASE BODY ASSEMBLY

1. With right sides together, sew the Fabric A bottom front rectangle 4″ × 23″ to the quilted front. Press the seam toward the quilted front.

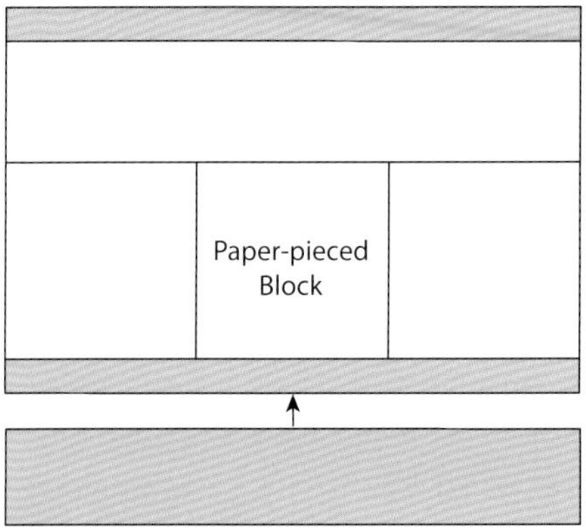

Bottom front added

2. Lay out 3 pillowcase layers in front of you, matching their 23″ edges as follows:

   A. Lining right side up (if there is a right side)

   B. Fabric A rectangle 23″ × 25¼″ right side up

   C. Quilted front wrong side up, matching its 23″ top edge to the other 2 layers

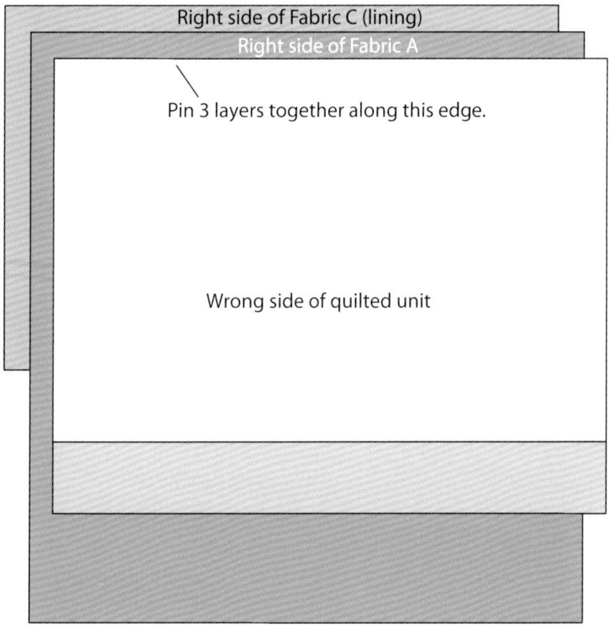

Pillowcase layers

3. Sew through all 3 layers.

LINING

1 Press the lining and main fabric seams towards the quilted front.

2 Fold the lining over the wrong side of the quilted unit. Press the lining's bottom edge under ¼″, or just where the lining will meet the stitching. On the wrong side, hand sew the lining to the seamline of the quilted front. The lining should neatly cover all of the raw seams.

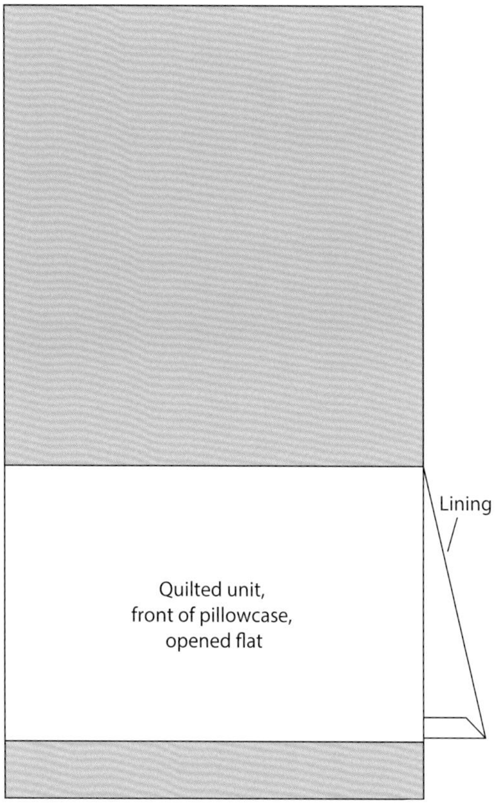

Lining to be hand-stitched to back of quilted front

ADD THE CUFF

Pin the WOF edge of the Fabric B 10″ strip to the long side edge of the pillowcase, right sides together. Trim the WOF cuff to fit the pillowcase perfectly.

"WEENIE ROLL" PILLOWCASE

1 Roll the side of the pillowcase *opposite* the cuff into a tube that will fit inside the cuff fabric.

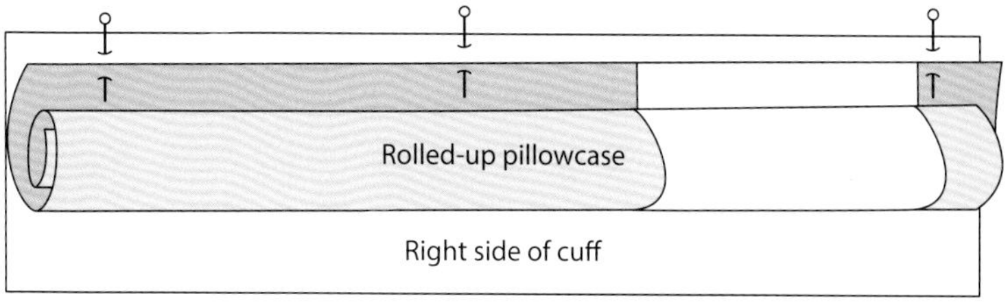

2 Flip the bottom of the cuff fabric over the top of the rolled fabric and pin over the top of the previously pinned edge. (It should look like a weenie inside of a tube.) Sew all layers together along the pinned edge.

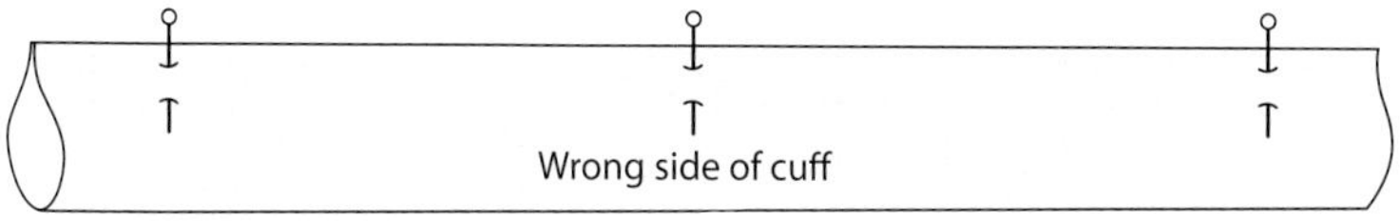

3 Pull the "roll" out through a side hole, and the cuff will turn right side out. Press the cuff flat. No visible seams!

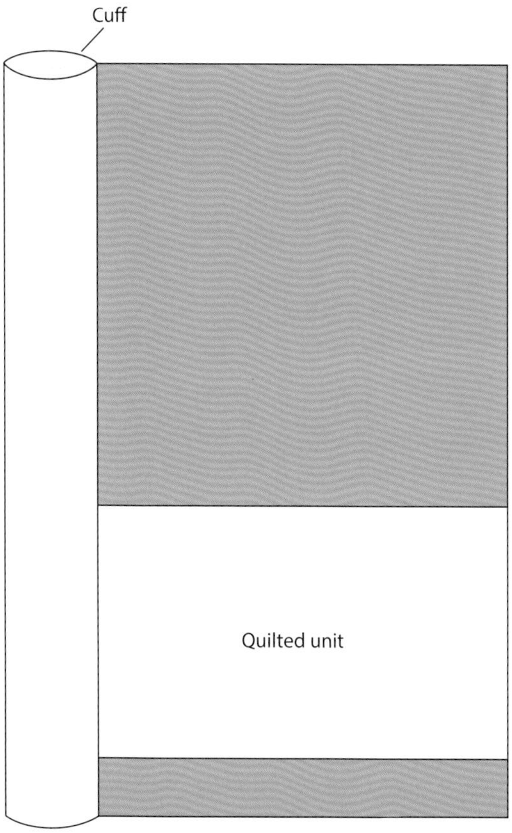

Finished cuff

SEW THE FRENCH SIDE SEAMS

Using the French seam method, there will be no exposed seams inside the pillowcase.

1. Fold the pillowcase in half with the *wrong* sides together.
2. Pin the bottom and side edges of the pillowcase.
3. Sew, using a ⅛″ seam allowance.

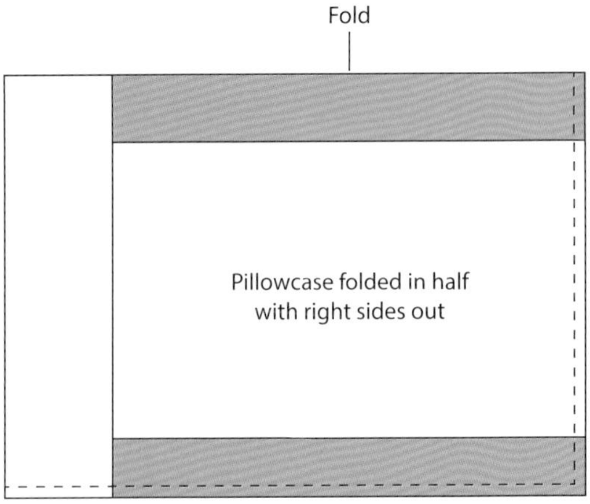

French seam along 2 edges

4. Turn the pillowcase *wrong* side out. *Gently* push the corners square. Press flat.
5. Pin the same 2 edges as in Step 2, but this time with *right* sides together.
6. Sew, using a ¼″ seam allowance. This seam encases the previous seam.
7. Turn the pillowcase right side out and press flat.

THROW PILLOW

FINISHED SIZE: 13″ × 13″ × 4″

A small throw pillow is so versatile. Toss it on a chair, sofa, or bed.

MATERIALS

Fabric requirements are based on 40″-wide fabric.

Fabric A: ½ yard for outer border and pillow back (*Note:* Use nondirectional fabric.)

Fabric B: ⅛ yard for inner border

Fabric C: ½ yard for lining (Muslin is recommended.)

Assorted scraps: To paper piece 1 block

Batting: 14″ × 14″ square

Pillow form: 12″ × 12″

Assorted buttons

Black embroidery floss

CUTTING

Fold fabric selvage to selvage for WOF (width of fabric) cuts unless otherwise directed.

Fabric A

For outer borders:

- Cut 2 strips 3″ × WOF. Subcut into 2 strips 3″ × 9″ and 2 strips 3″ × 13″.

For pillow back:

- Cut 1 strip 9″ × WOF. Subcut into 2 rectangles 9″ × 13½″.

Fabric B

- Cut 1 strip 1″ × WOF. Subcut into 2 strips 1″ × 8″ and 2 strips 1″ × 9″.

Fabric C

Open fabric flat.

- Cut 1 square 14″ × 14″ for lining.

Batting

- Cut 1 square 14″ × 14″.

Sewing

Use ¼″ seams throughout, unless otherwise directed.

PAPER-PIECED BLOCK

Refer to Paper-Piecing Basics (page 7) as needed. Refer to Block Patterns (pages 37–53) to choose blocks.

1. Paper piece 1 selected block, using the assorted scraps.

2. Add any necessary embroidery to the blocks. Do not add any buttons at this time, but mark their placement. If this pillow is to be used for a baby, appliqué fabric circles for the eyes instead of using buttons, which might be a choking hazard.

3. Trim the block to 8″ × 8″.

ADD THE SASHING

1. Sew the shorter (8″) Fabric B strips to the top and bottom of the paper-pieced block. Press the seams away from the block.

2. Sew the longer (9″) Fabric B strips to the sides of the block. Press the seams away from the block. The pillow front should now measure 9″ × 9″.

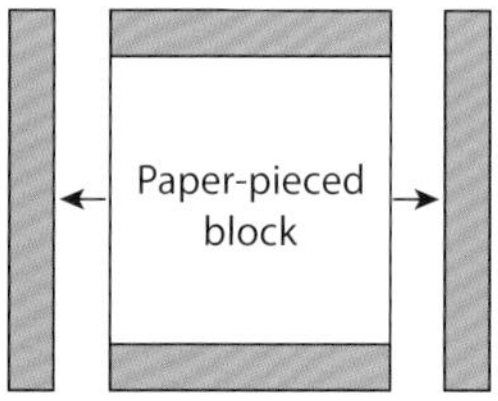

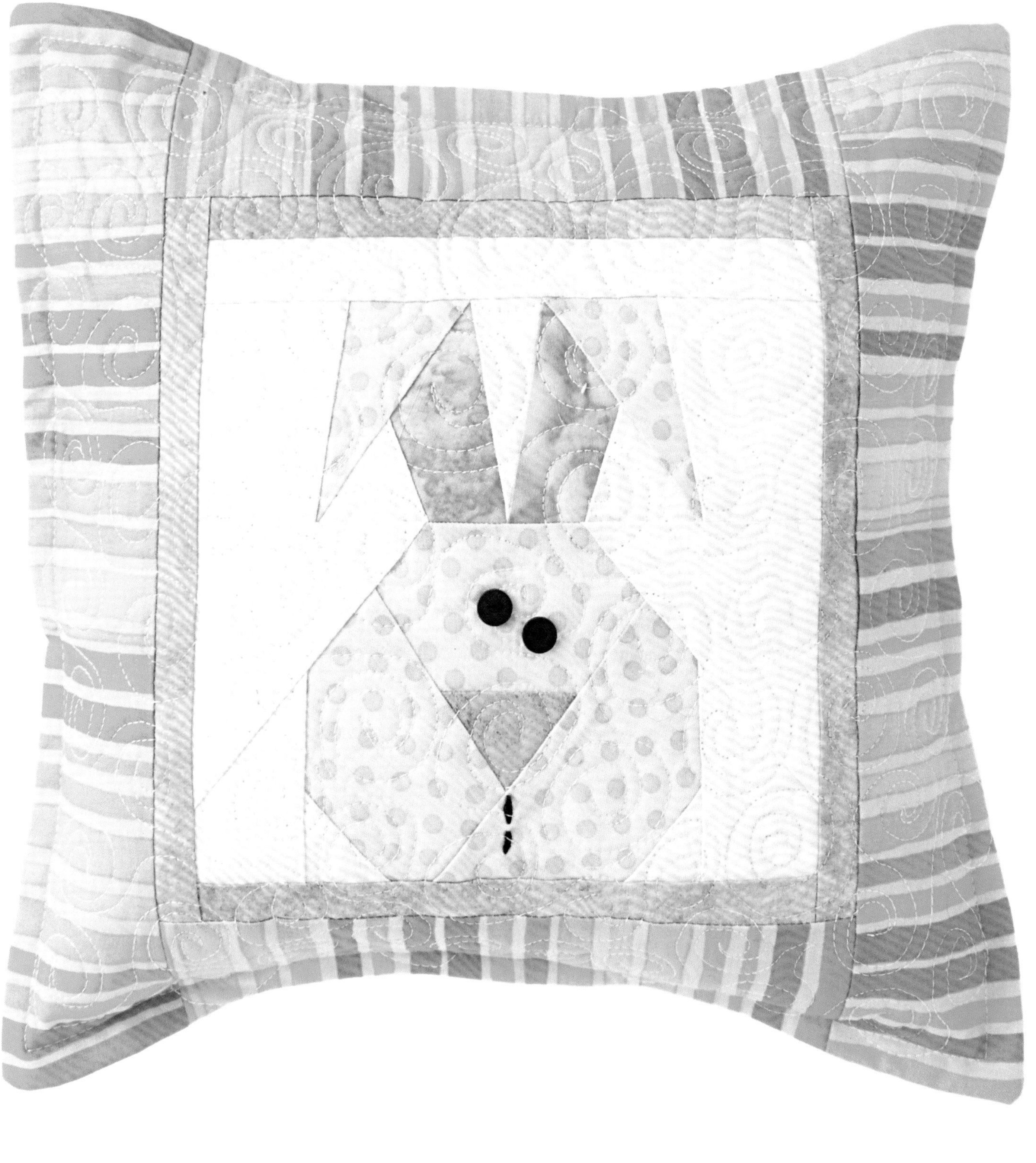

ADD THE BORDER

1 Sew the shorter (9″) Fabric A outer borders to the top and bottom of the pillow front, as in Add the Sashing, Step 1 (page 34). Press the seams away from the sashing.

2 Sew the longer (13″) Fabric A outer borders to the sides of the pillow front, as in Add the Sashing, Step 2 (page 34). Press the seams away from the sashing.

QUILT THE PILLOW FRONT

1 Remove the paper from the back of the paper-pieced block.

2 Layer the pillow front (right side facing up), batting, and lining (right side facing down). The batting and lining will be slightly larger than the pillow front at this stage. Pin or baste together. Quilt as desired.

3 Trim the pillow front to 13½″ × 13½″.

4 Hand sew any necessary buttons to the paper-pieced blocks, sewing through all thicknesses.

PREPARE THE PILLOW BACK

1 Press the raw edges under ½″ on a 13½″ side of each Fabric A pillow back.

2 Press under another ½″ on the same side and topstitch these pressed edges to form a hem along one edge of each pillow back.

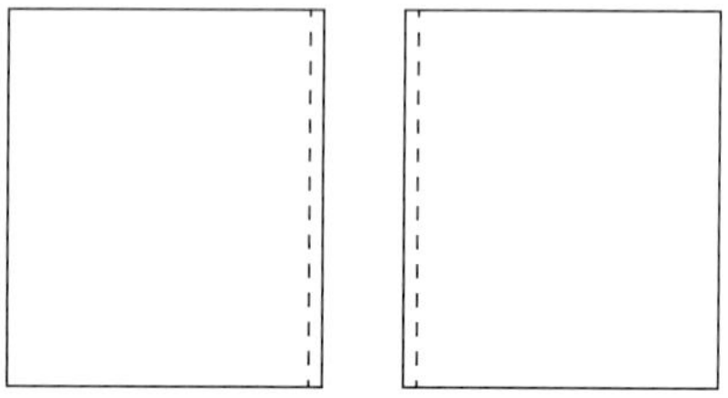

Hemmed pillow backs

3 With the right sides facing down, overlap the hemmed edges of the 2 backs by approximately 1¼″, so the total shape of the pillow back measures 13½″ × 13½″. Pin the rectangles together where they overlap, on the wrong side of the fabric.

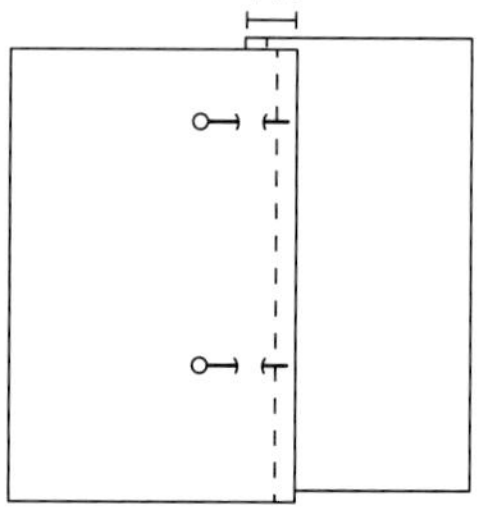

Pillow backs overlapped

ASSEMBLE THE PILLOW

1 Pin the pillow front to the pillow back, right sides together.

2 Sew, using a ¼″ seam allowance around all 4 sides of the pillow.

3 Remove the pins and turn the pillow right side out, gently pushing out the corners. Press the edges flat.

4 Topstitch ½″ from the edge of the pillow.

FINISHING

Slide the 12″ × 12″ pillow form through the back opening. The pillow will have a nice, snug fit.

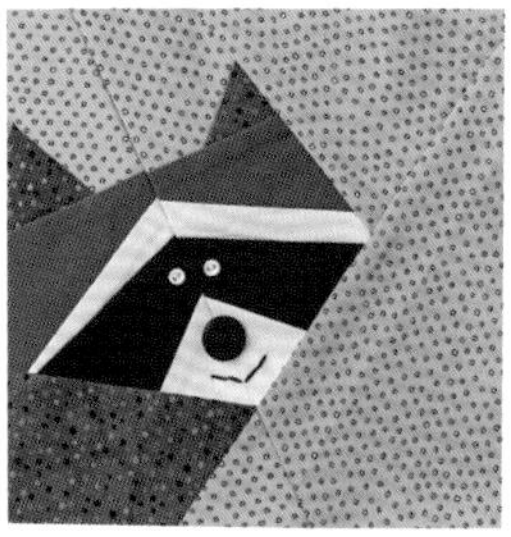

BLOCK PATTERNS

All block patterns are 7½″ square but are trimmed to 8″ square to allow for ¼″ seam allowances. Refer to Paper-Piecing Basics (page 7) as needed when making the blocks.

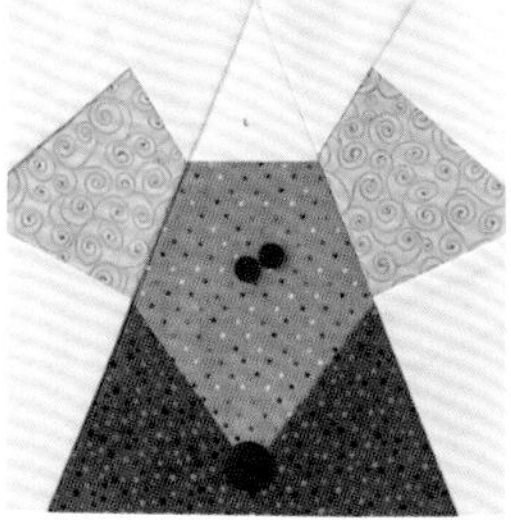

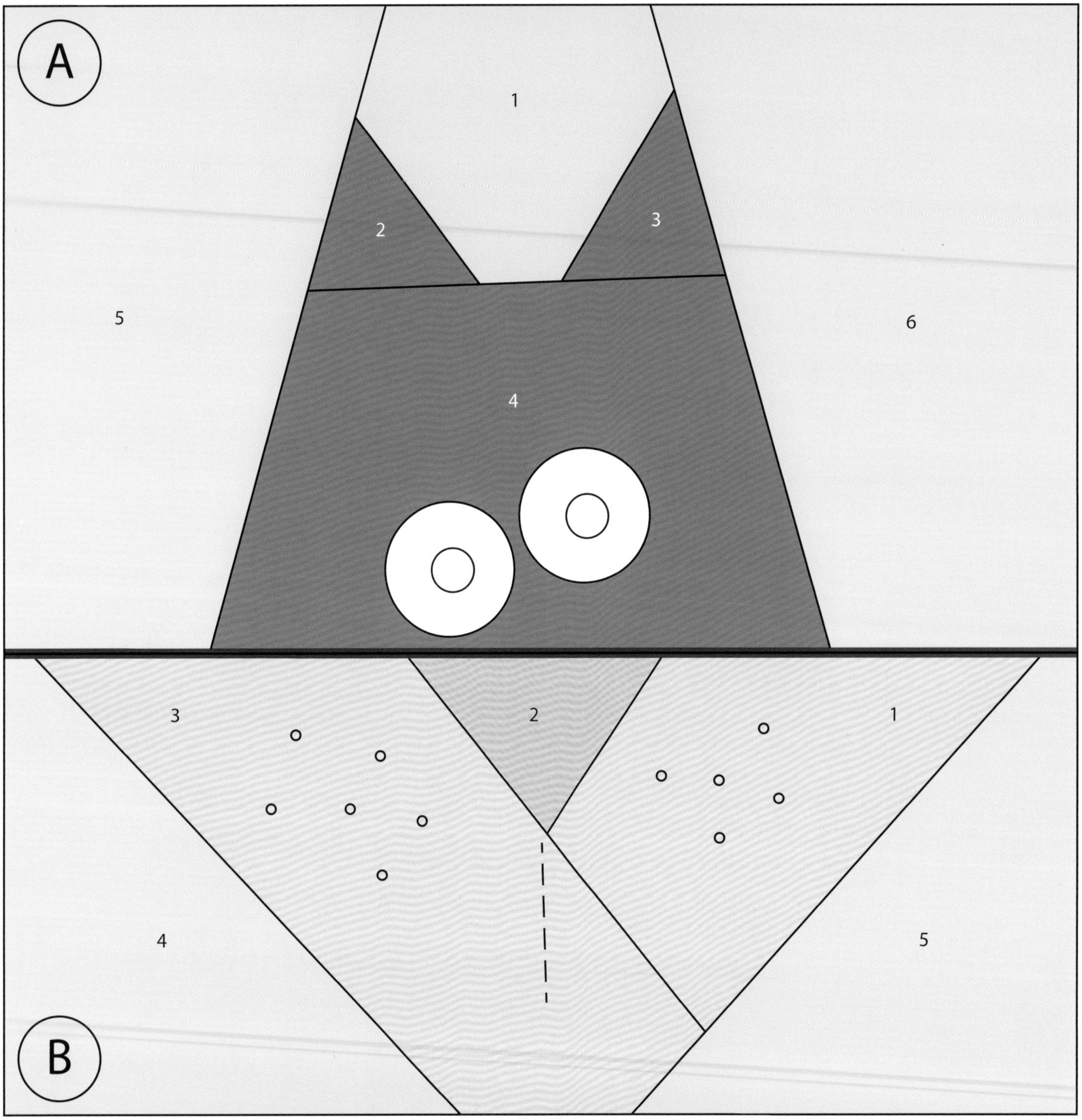

CAT 1

MATERIALS

- Large scrap of blue, at least 9″ × 11″
- Scraps of black, gray, and pink
- 2 white ⅞″ buttons and 2 black ¼″ buttons for eyes
- Black embroidery floss

DIRECTIONS

For detailed directions, refer to Paper-Piecing Basics (page 7).

1. Make 2 copies of the pattern (A, B).
2. Cut around each segment, adding ¼″ seam allowances.
3. Paper piece each segment.
4. Connect the segments: A to B.
5. Embroider the mouth and freckles with the paper still attached.
6. Trim the block to 8″ × 8″.

When directed in the project instructions, remove the paper from the back of the block and hand sew any buttons on.

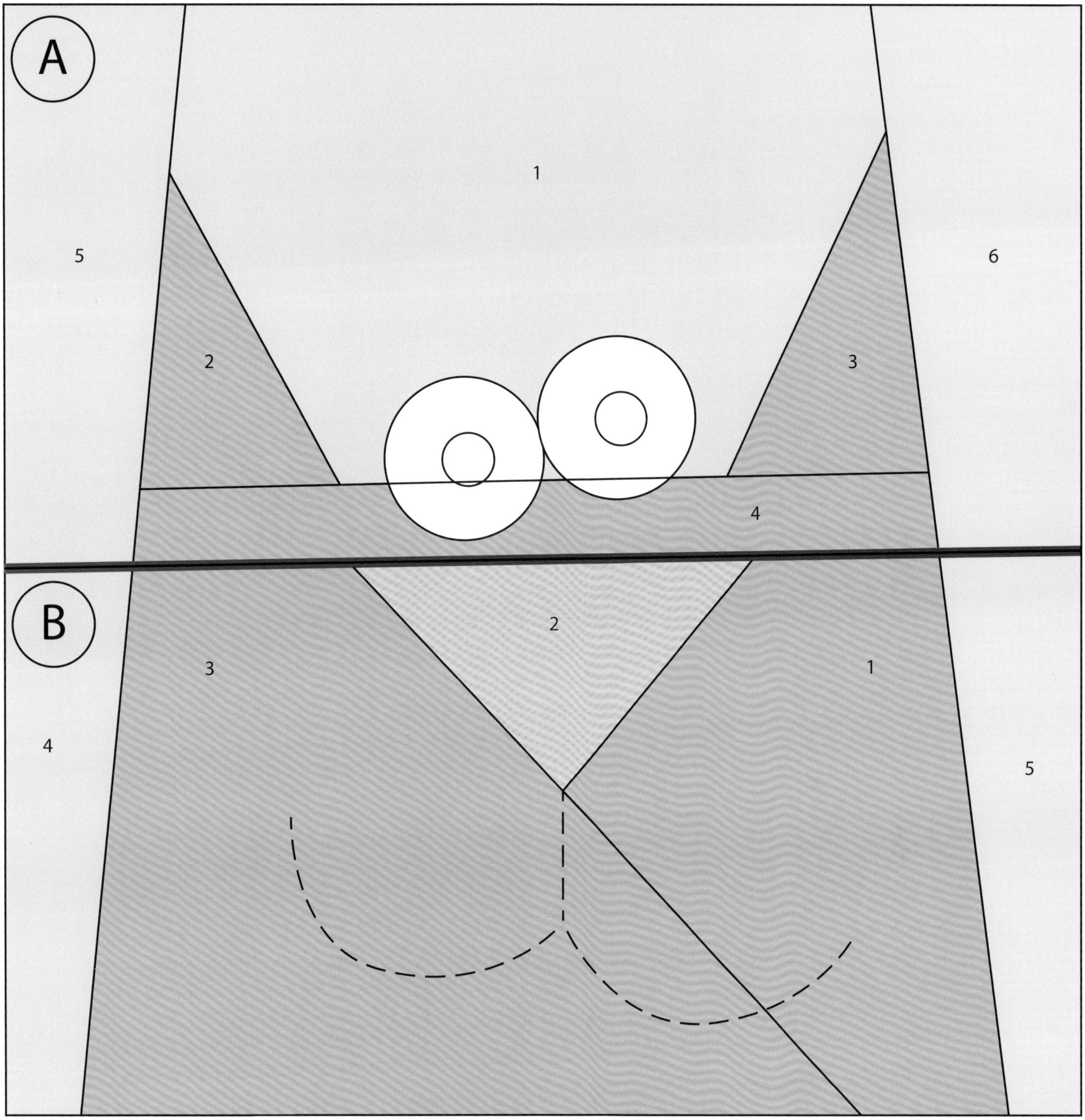

CAT 2

MATERIALS

- Large scrap of blue, at least 9″ × 11″
- Scraps of gray and pink
- 2 white 1″ buttons and 2 black ¼″ buttons for eyes
- Black embroidery floss

DIRECTIONS

For detailed directions, refer to Paper-Piecing Basics (page 7).

1. Make 2 copies of the pattern (A, B).
2. Cut around each segment, adding ¼″ seam allowances.
3. Paper piece each segment.
4. Connect the segments: A to B.
5. Embroider the mouth with the paper still attached.
6. Trim the block to 8″ × 8″.

When directed in the project instructions, remove the paper from the back of the block and hand sew any buttons on.

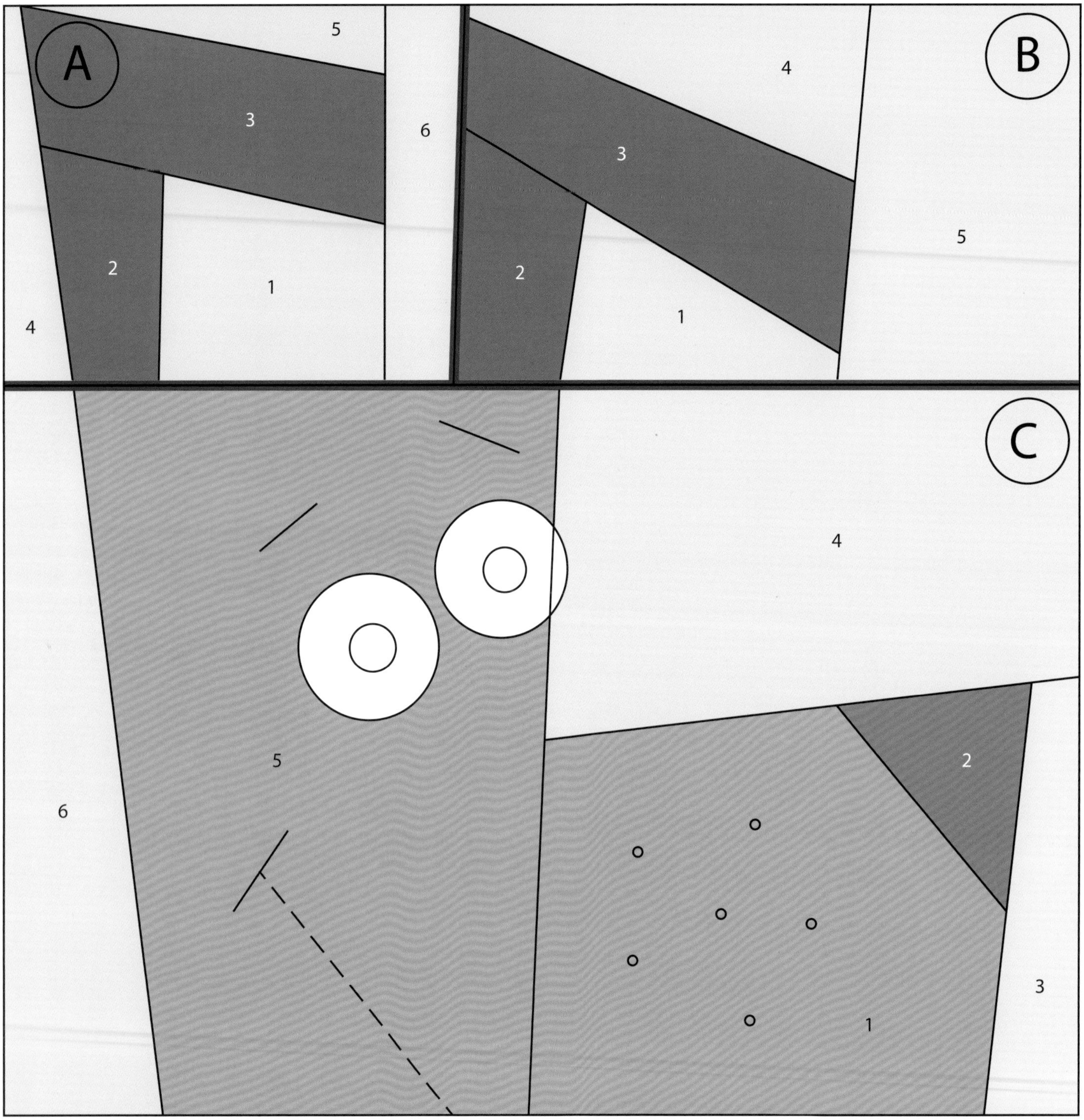

DOG 1

MATERIALS

- Large scrap of blue, at least 9″ × 11″
- Scraps of light brown, dark brown, and black
- 2 white 1″ buttons and 2 black ¼″ buttons for eyes
- Black embroidery floss

DIRECTIONS

For detailed directions, refer to Paper-Piecing Basics (page 7).

1. Make 3 copies of the pattern (A, B, C).
2. Cut around each segment, adding ¼″ seam allowances.
3. Paper piece each segment.
4. Connect the segments: A to B; A/B to C.
5. Embroider the mouth, freckles, and eyebrows with the paper still attached.
6. Trim the block to 8″ × 8″.

When directed in the project instructions, remove the paper from the back of the block and hand sew any buttons on.

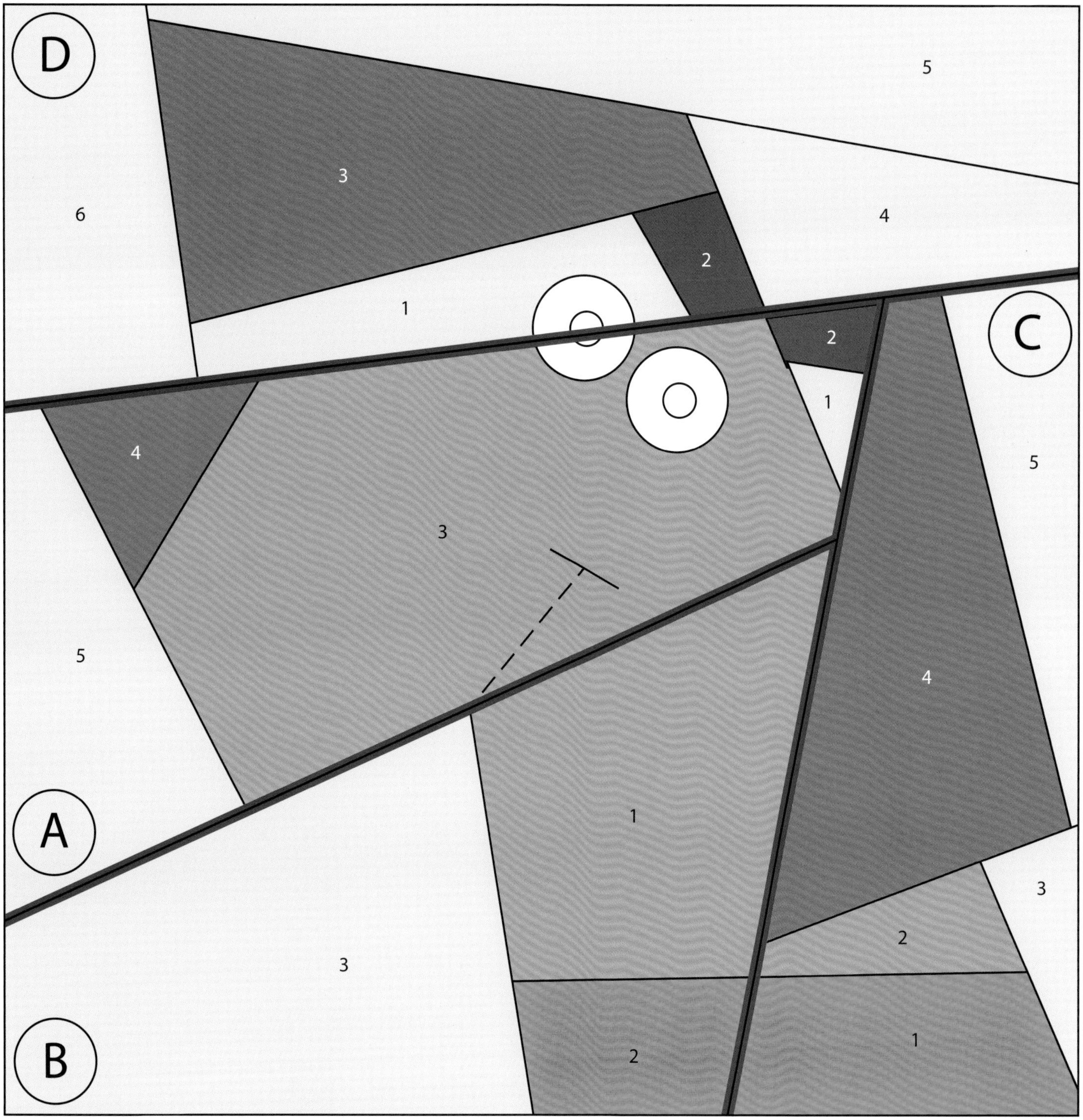

DOG 2

MATERIALS

- Large scrap of blue, at least 9″ × 11″
- Scraps of light brown, dark brown, very dark brown, black, and red
- 2 white ¾″ buttons and 2 black ¼″ buttons for eyes
- Black embroidery floss

DIRECTIONS

For detailed directions, refer to Paper-Piecing Basics (page 7).

1. Make 3 copies of the pattern (A, B/D, C).
2. Cut around each segment, adding ¼″ seam allowances.
3. Paper piece each segment.
4. Connect the segments: A to B; A/B to C; A/B/C to D.
5. Embroider the mouth with the paper still attached.
6. Trim the block to 8″ × 8″.

When directed in the project instructions, remove the paper from the back of the block and hand sew any buttons on.

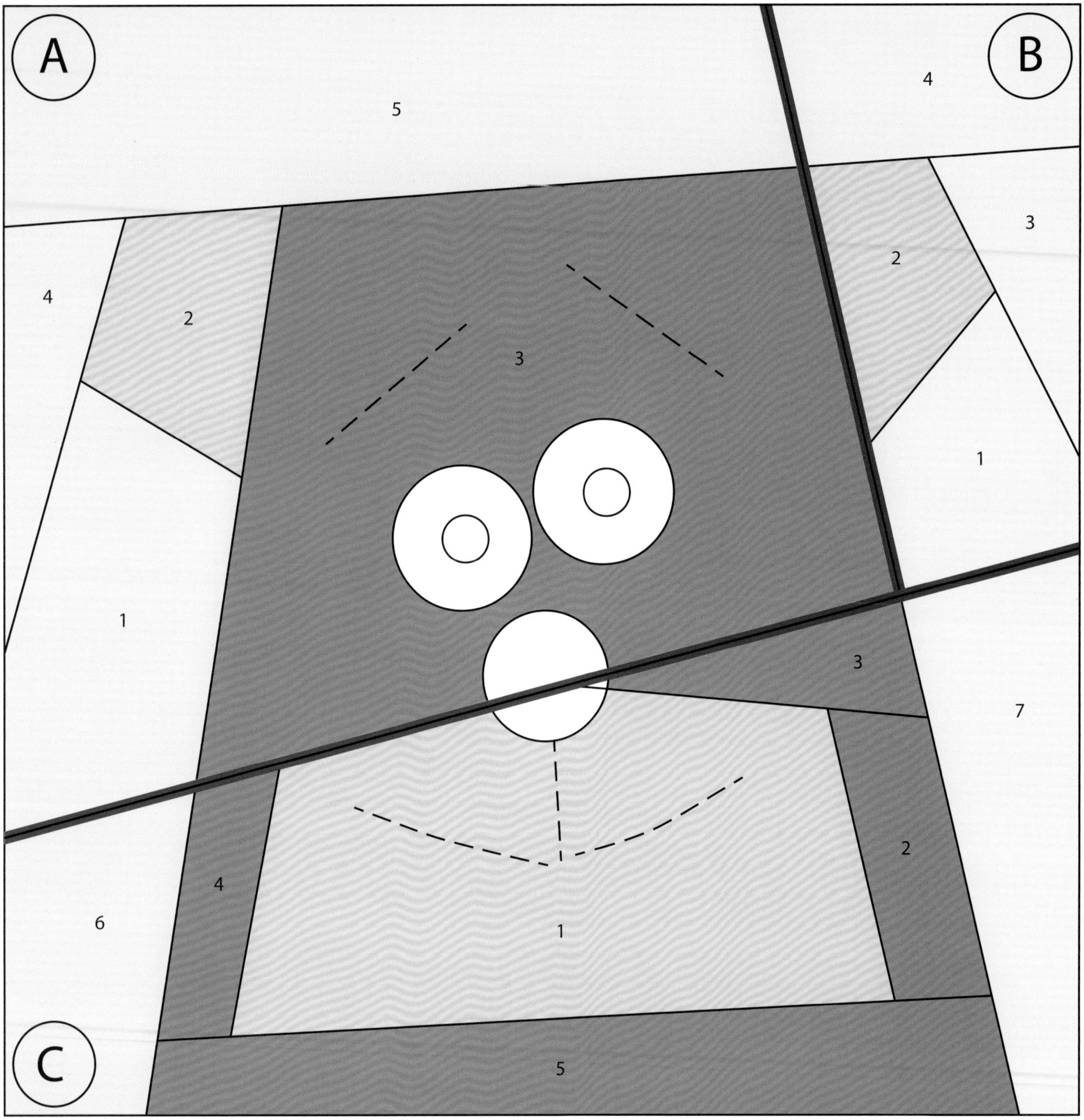

BEAR

MATERIALS

- Large scrap of blue, at least 9″ × 11″
- Scraps of light brown and medium brown
- 2 white 1″ buttons and 2 black ¼″ buttons for eyes
- 1 black ⅞″ button for nose
- Black embroidery floss

DIRECTIONS

For detailed directions, refer to Paper-Piecing Basics (page 7).

1. Make 3 copies of the pattern (A, B, C).

2. Cut around each segment, adding ¼″ seam allowances.

3. Paper piece each segment.

4. Connect the segments: A to B; A/B to C.

5. Embroider the mouth and eyebrows with the paper still attached.

6. Trim the block to 8″ × 8″.

When directed in the project instructions, remove the paper from the back of the block and hand sew any buttons on.

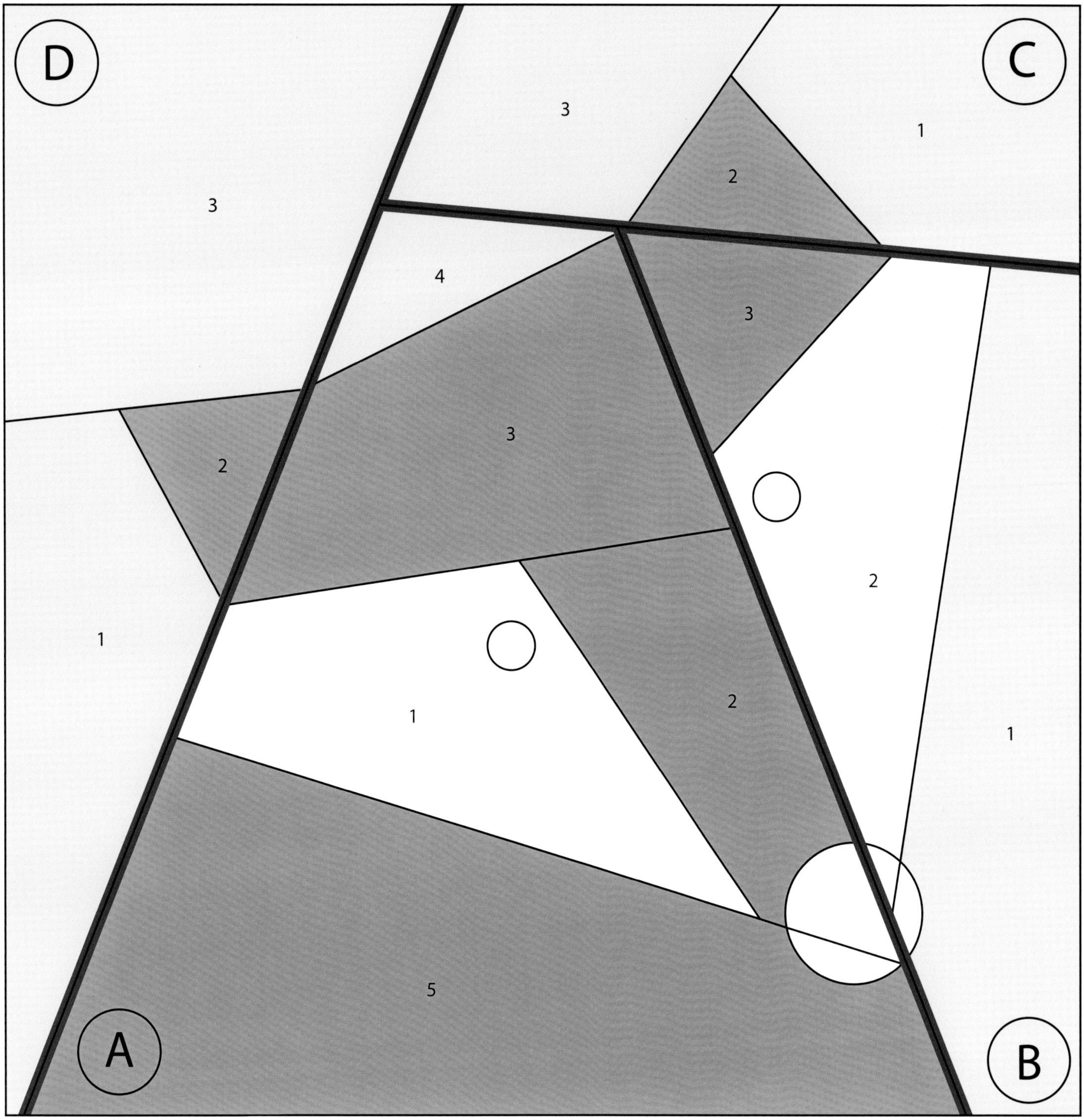

FOX

MATERIALS

- Large scrap of blue, at least 9″ × 11″
- Scraps of dark orange and white
- 2 black ¼″ buttons for eyes
- 1 black 1″ button for nose

DIRECTIONS

For detailed directions, refer to Paper-Piecing Basics (page 7).

1. Make 3 copies of the pattern (A, B/D, C).
2. Cut around each segment, adding ¼″ seam allowances.
3. Paper piece each segment.
4. Connect the segments: A to B; A/B to C; A/B/C to D.
5. Trim the block to 8″ × 8″.

When directed in the project instructions, remove the paper from the back of the block and hand sew any buttons on.

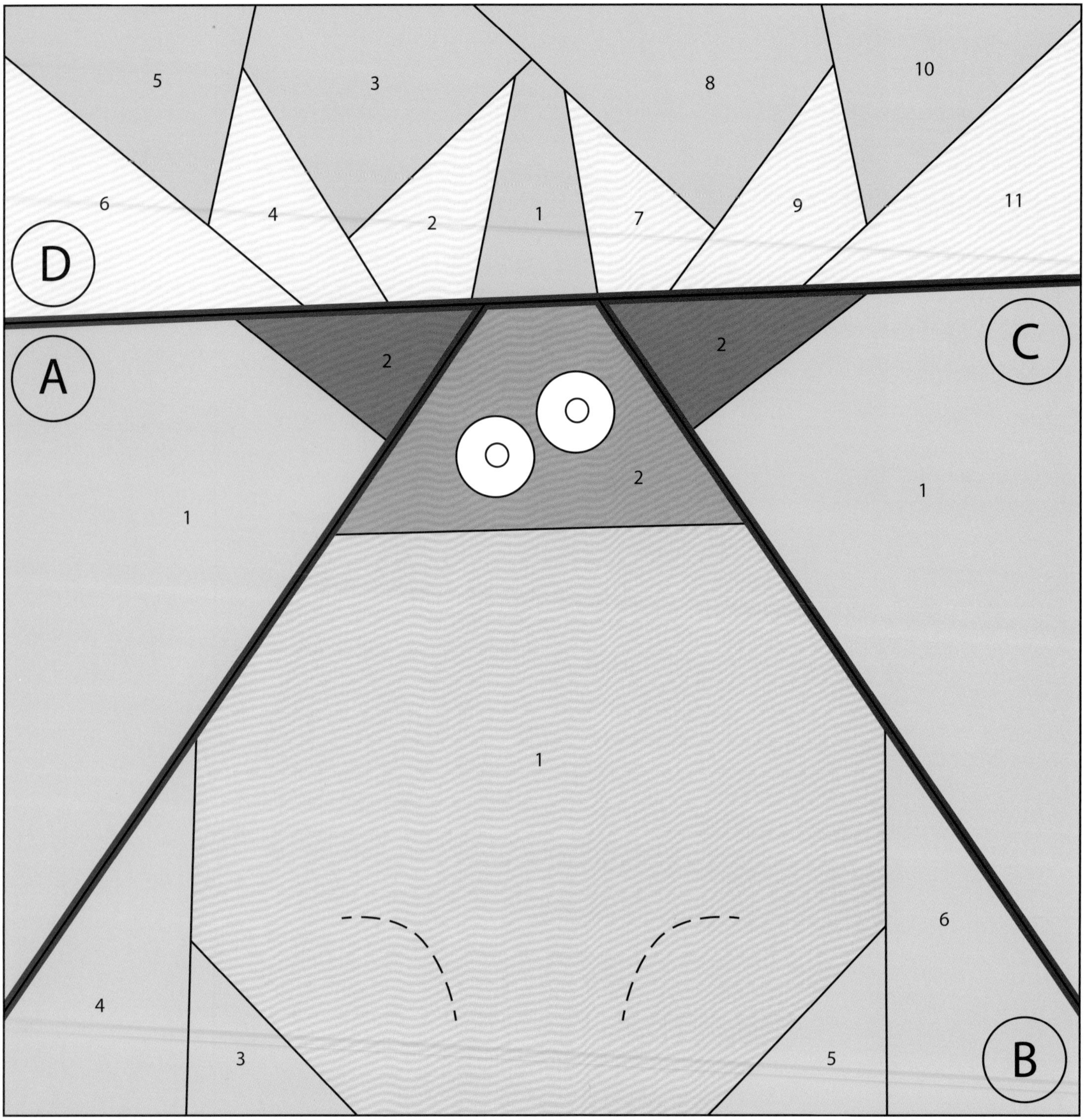

MOOSE

MATERIALS

- Large scrap of blue, at least 9″ × 11″
- Scraps of brown, medium brown, dark brown, and cream
- 2 white ⅝″ buttons and 2 black ⅛″ buttons for eyes
- Black embroidery floss

DIRECTIONS

For detailed directions, refer to Paper-Piecing Basics (page 7).

1. Make 3 copies of the pattern (A/C, B, D).
2. Cut around each segment, adding ¼″ seam allowances.
3. Paper piece each segment.
4. Connect the segments: A to B to C; A/B/C to D.
5. Embroider the nostrils with the paper still attached.
6. Trim the block to 8″ × 8″.

When directed in the project instructions, remove the paper from the back of the block and hand sew any buttons on.

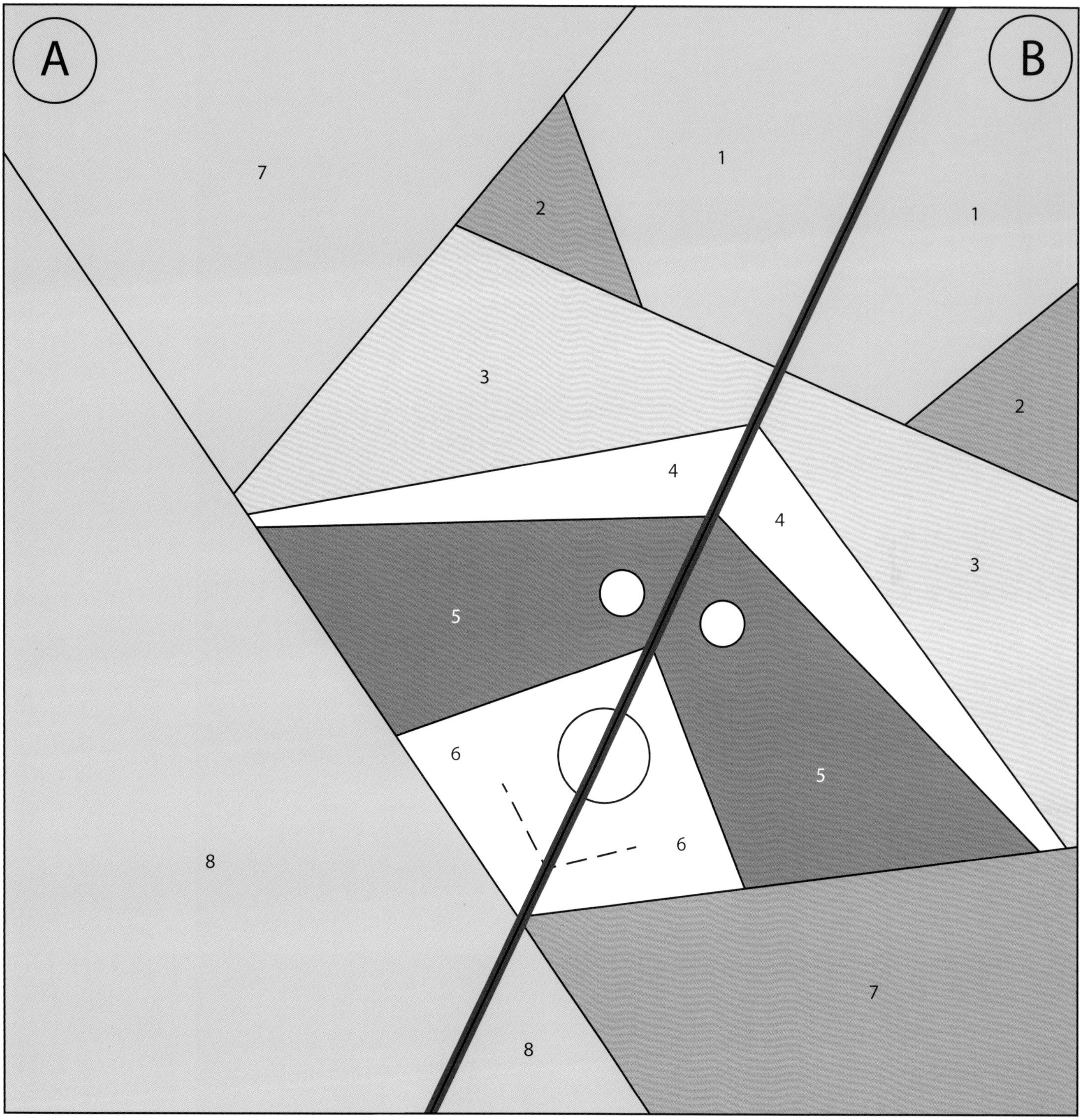

RACCOON

MATERIALS

- Large scrap of blue, at least 9″ × 11″
- Scraps of white, black, dark gray, and green-gray
- 2 white ¼″ buttons for eyes
- 1 black ⅝″ button for nose
- Black embroidery floss

DIRECTIONS

For detailed directions, refer to Paper-Piecing Basics (page 7).

1. Make 2 copies of the pattern (A, B).
2. Cut around each segment, adding ¼″ seam allowances.
3. Paper piece each segment.
4. Connect the segments: A to B.
5. Embroider the mouth with the paper still attached.
6. Trim the block to 8″ × 8″.

When directed in the project instructions, remove the paper from the back of the block and hand sew any buttons on.

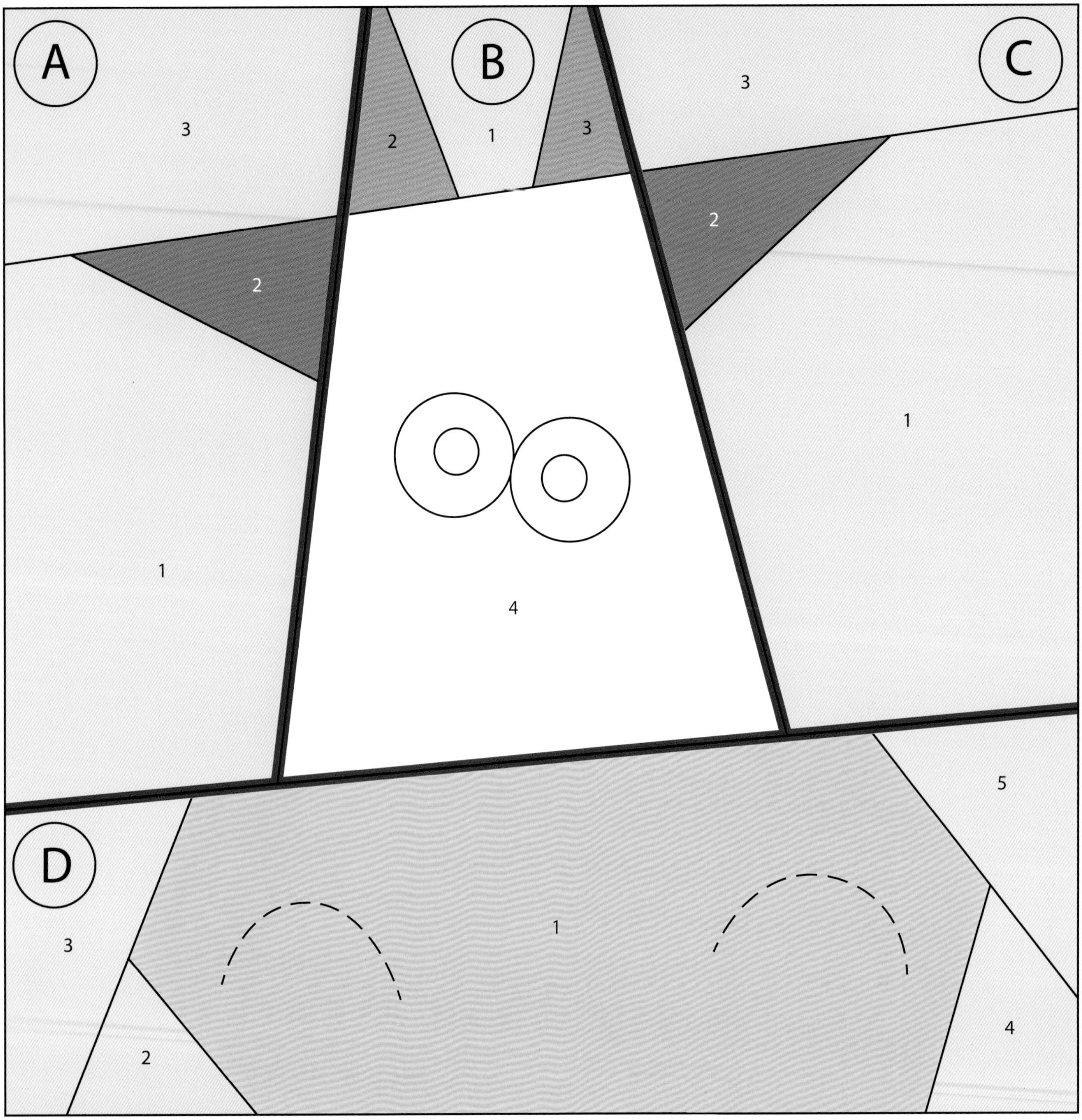

COW

MATERIALS

- Large scrap of blue, at least 9″ × 11″
- Scraps of peach, white-and-black print, gray, and black
- 2 white ¾″ buttons and 2 black ¼″ buttons for eyes
- Black embroidery floss

DIRECTIONS

For detailed directions, refer to Paper-Piecing Basics (page 7).

1. Make 3 copies of the pattern (A/C, B, D).
2. Cut around each segment, adding ¼″ seam allowances.
3. Paper piece each segment.
4. Connect the segments: A to B to C; A/B/C to D.
5. Embroider the nostrils with the paper still attached.
6. Trim the block to 8″ × 8″.

When directed in the project instructions, remove the paper from the back of the block and hand sew any buttons on.

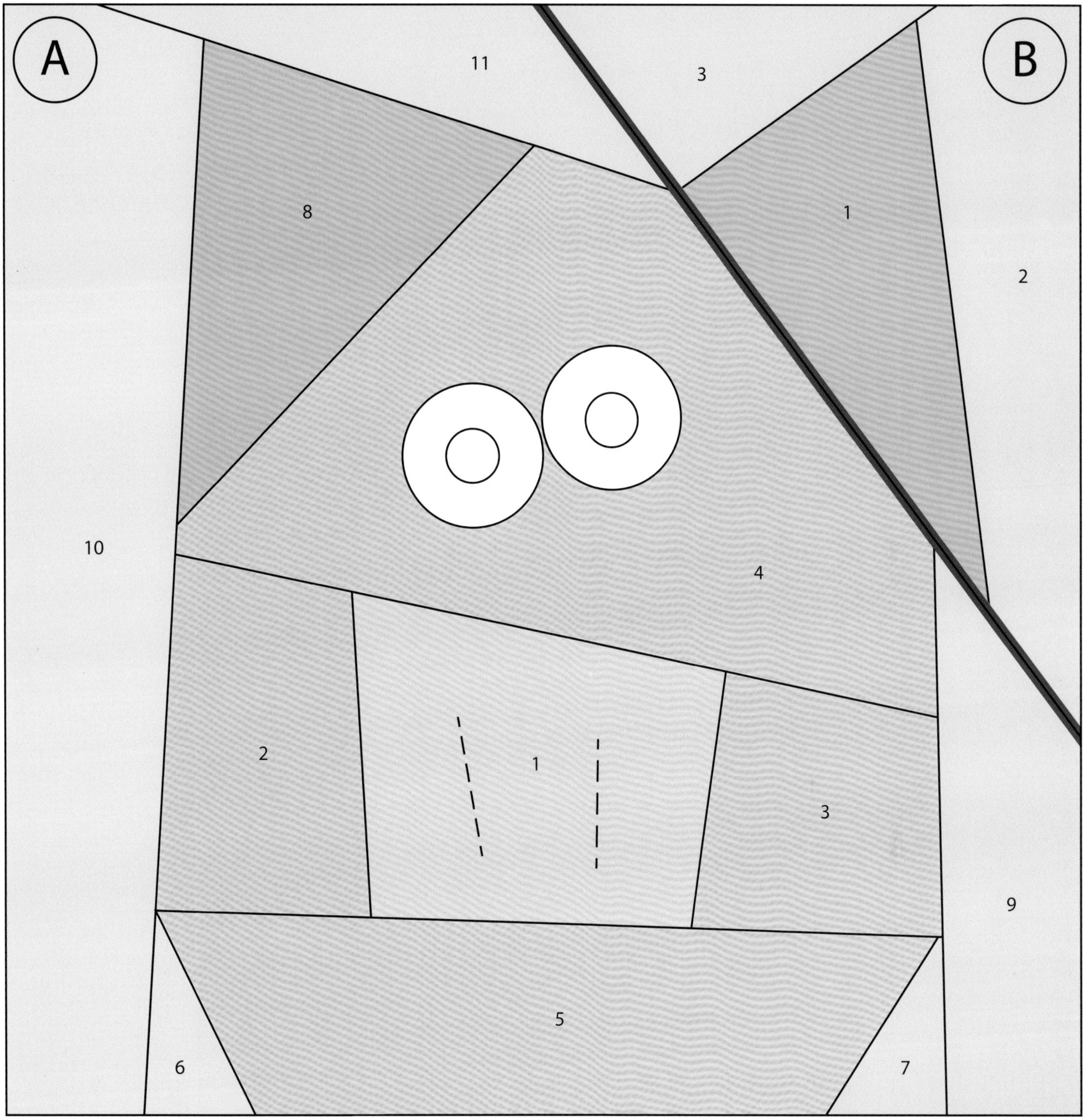

PIG

MATERIALS

- Large scrap of blue, at least 9″ × 11″
- Scraps of pink, light gray, and purple
- 2 white 1″ buttons and 2 black ¼″ buttons for eyes
- Black embroidery floss

DIRECTIONS

For detailed directions, refer to Paper-Piecing Basics (page 7).

1. Make 2 copies of the pattern (A, B).
2. Cut around each segment, adding ¼″ seam allowances.
3. Paper piece each segment.
4. Connect the segments: A to B.
5. Embroider the nostrils with the paper still attached.
6. Trim the block to 8″ × 8″.

When directed in the project instructions, remove the paper from the back of the block and hand sew any buttons on.

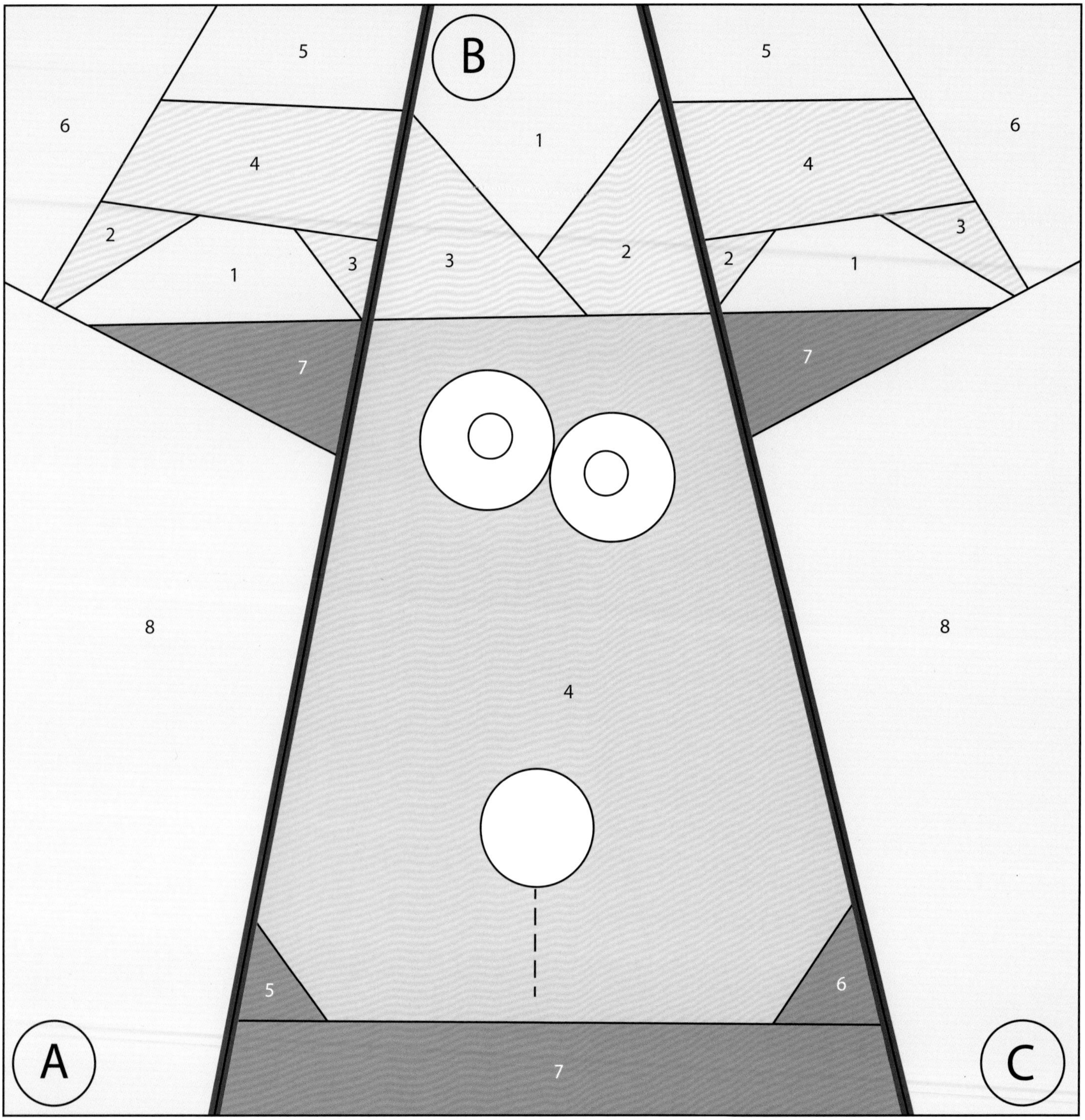

GOAT

MATERIALS

- Large scrap of blue, at least 9″ × 11″
- Scraps of light gray, dark gray, and tan
- 2 white 1″ buttons and 2 black ¼″ buttons for eyes
- 1 black ¾″ button for nose
- Black embroidery floss

DIRECTIONS

For detailed directions, refer to Paper-Piecing Basics (page 7).

1. Make 2 copies of the pattern (A/C, B).
2. Cut around each segment, adding ¼″ seam allowances.
3. Paper piece each segment.
4. Connect the segments: A to B; A/B to C.
5. Embroider the mouth with the paper still attached.
6. Trim the block to 8″ × 8″.

When directed in the project instructions, remove the paper from the back of the block and hand sew any buttons on.

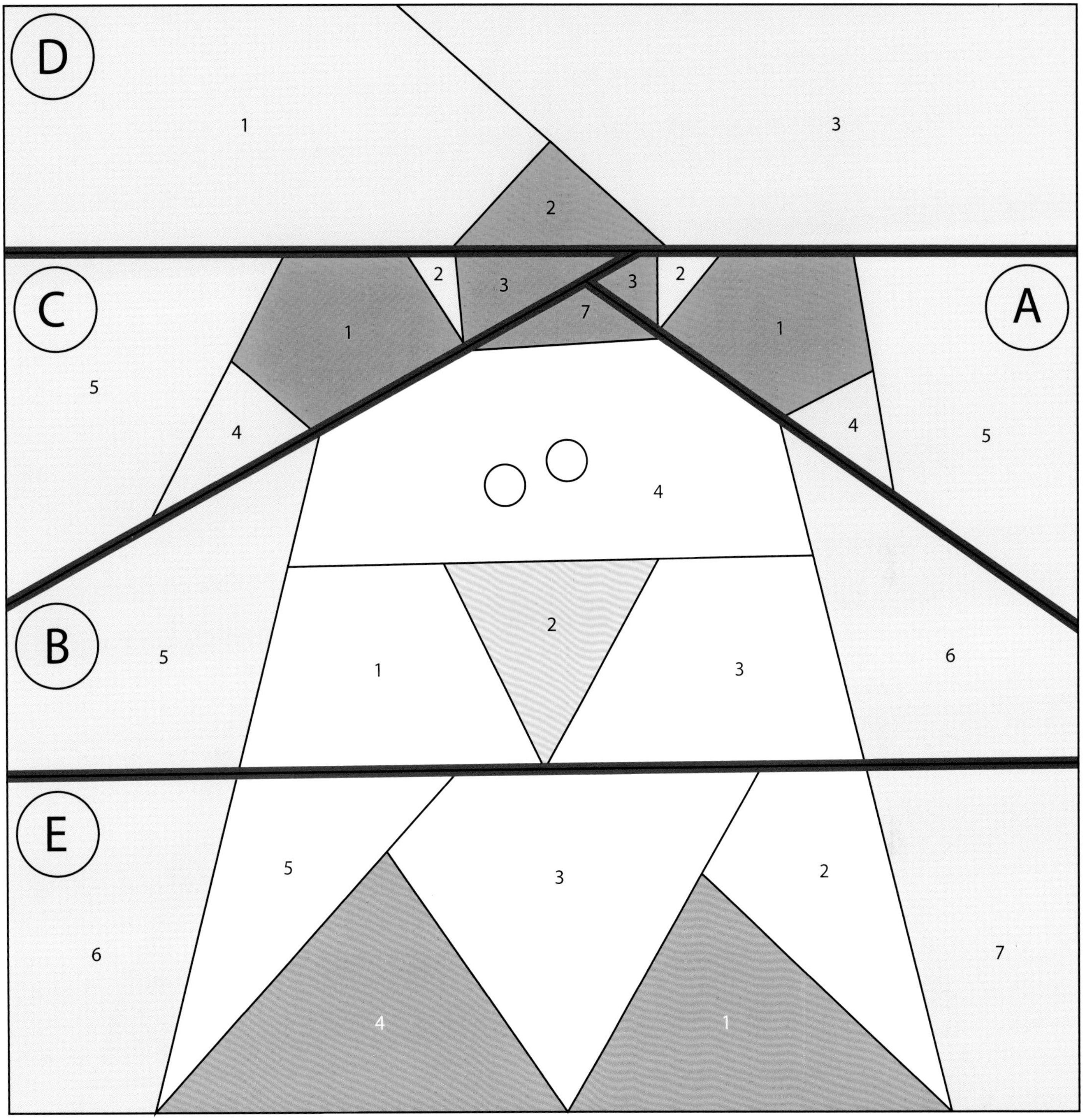

CHICKEN

MATERIALS

- Large scrap of blue, at least 9″ × 11″
- Scraps of white, light brown, red, and yellow
- 2 black ¼″ buttons for eyes

DIRECTIONS

For detailed directions, refer to Paper-Piecing Basics (page 7).

1. Make 3 copies of the pattern (A/E, B/D, C).
2. Cut around each segment, adding ¼″ seam allowances.
3. Paper piece each segment.
4. Connect the segments: A to B; A/B to C; A/B/C to D and E.
5. Trim the block to 8″ × 8″.

When directed in the project instructions, remove the paper from the back of the block and hand sew any buttons on.

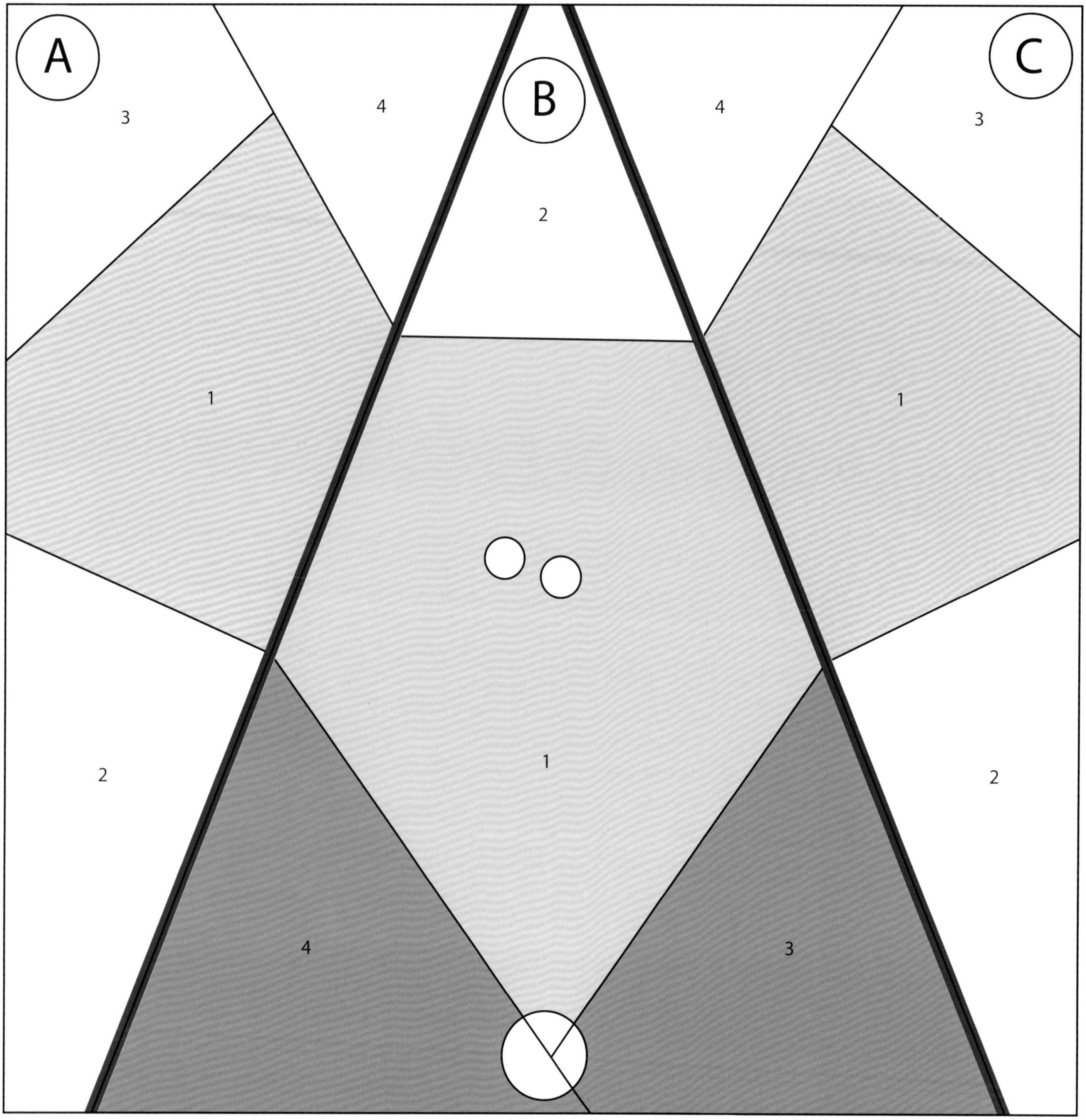

MOUSE

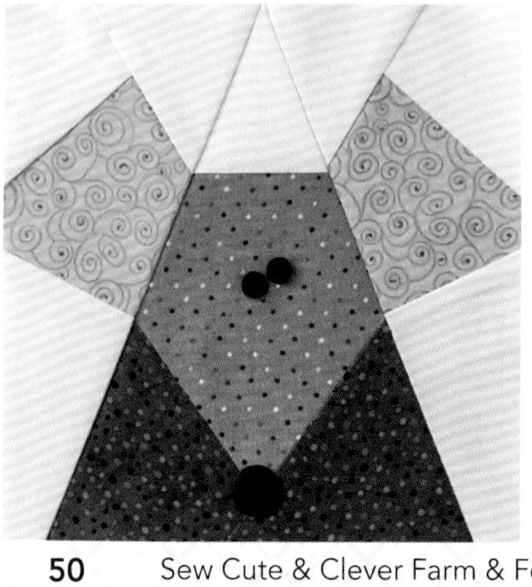

Materials

- Large scrap of white, at least 9″ × 11″
- Scraps of light gray, dark gray, and pink
- 2 black ¼″ buttons for eyes
- 1 black ⅝″ button for nose

Directions

For detailed directions, refer to Paper-Piecing Basics (page 7).

1. Make 2 copies of the pattern (A/C, B).
2. Cut around each segment, adding ¼″ seam allowances.
3. Paper piece each segment.
4. Connect the segments: A to B; A/B to C.
5. Trim the block to 8″ × 8″.

When directed in the project instructions, remove the paper from the back of the block and hand sew any buttons on.

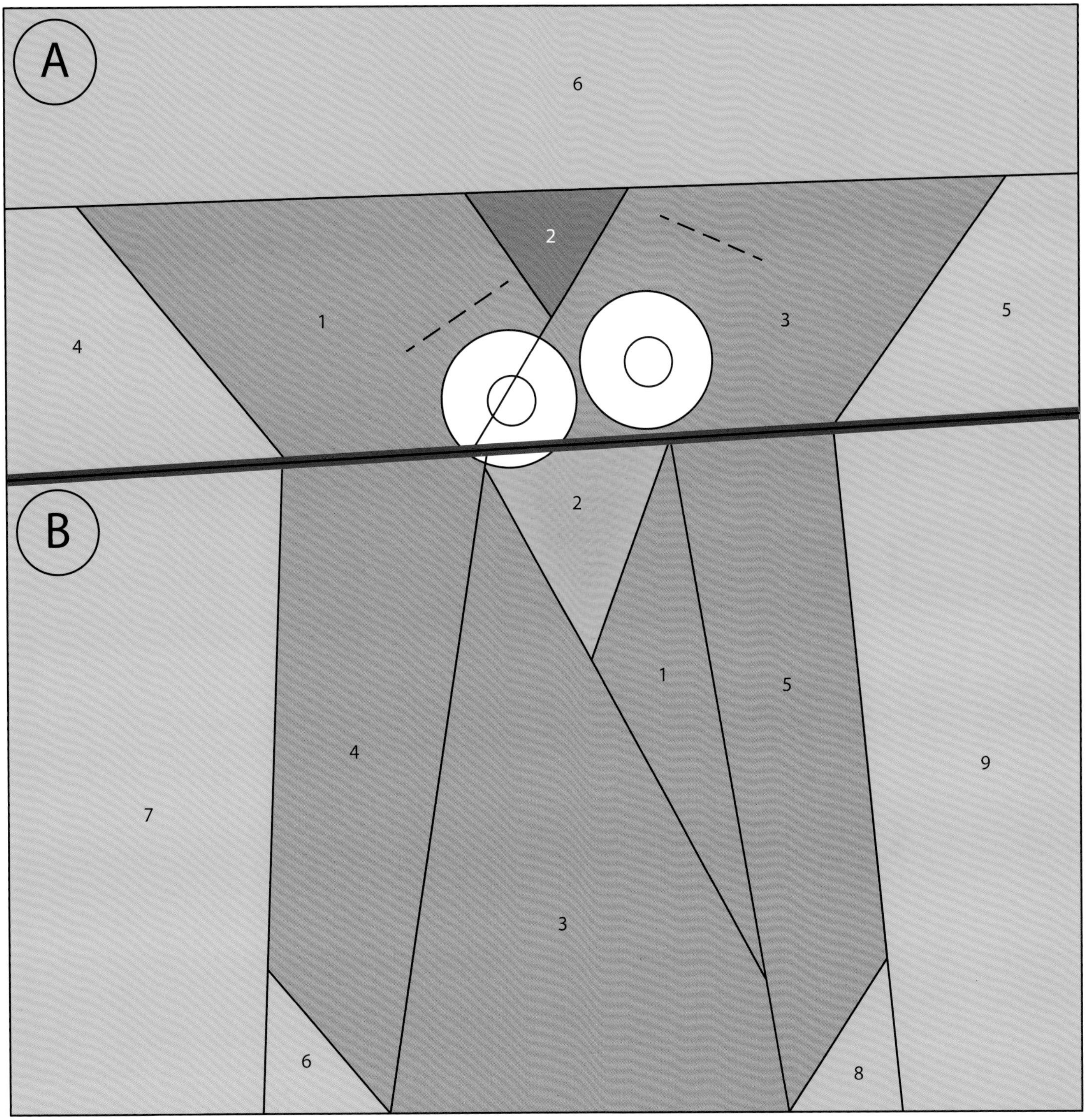

OWL

MATERIALS

- Large scrap of blue, at least 9″ × 11″
- Scraps of gray, brown, orange, and black
- 2 white ⅞″ buttons and 2 black ¼″ buttons for eyes
- Black embroidery floss

DIRECTIONS

For detailed directions, refer to Paper-Piecing Basics (page 7).

1. Make 2 copies of the pattern (A, B).
2. Cut around each segment, adding ¼″ seam allowances.
3. Paper piece each segment.
4. Connect the segments: A to B.
5. Embroider the eyebrows with the paper still attached.
6. Trim the block to 8″ × 8″.

When directed in the project instructions, remove the paper from the back of the block and hand sew any buttons on.

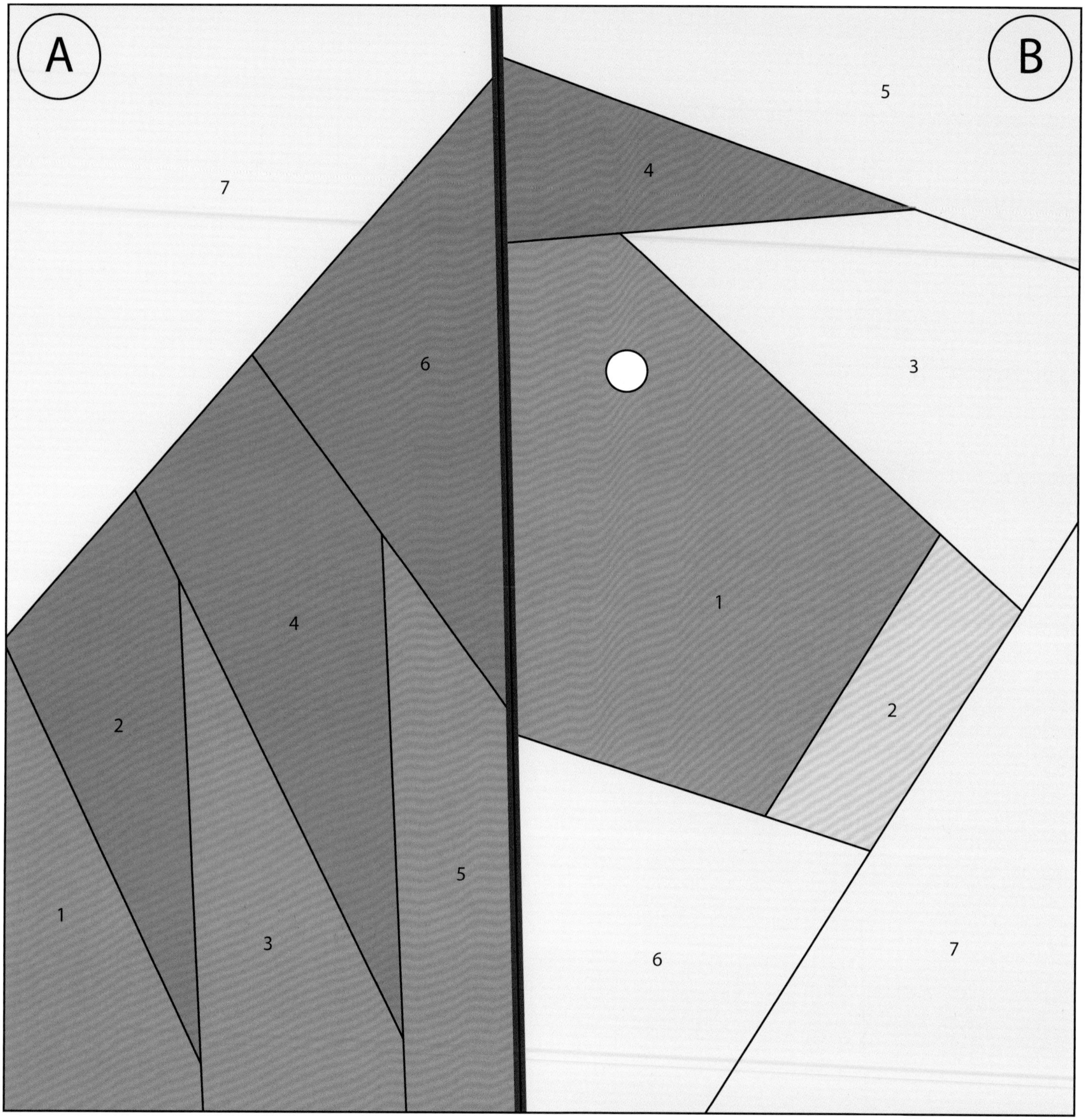

PONY

MATERIALS

- Large scrap of blue, at least 9″ × 11″
- Scraps of light brown, medium brown, and black
- 1 black ¼″ button for eye

DIRECTIONS

For detailed directions, refer to Paper-Piecing Basics (page 7).

1. Make 2 copies of the pattern (A, B).
2. Cut around each segment, adding ¼″ seam allowances.
3. Paper piece each segment.
4. Connect the segments: A to B.
5. Trim the block to 8″ × 8″.

When directed in the project instructions, remove the paper from the back of the block and hand sew any buttons on.

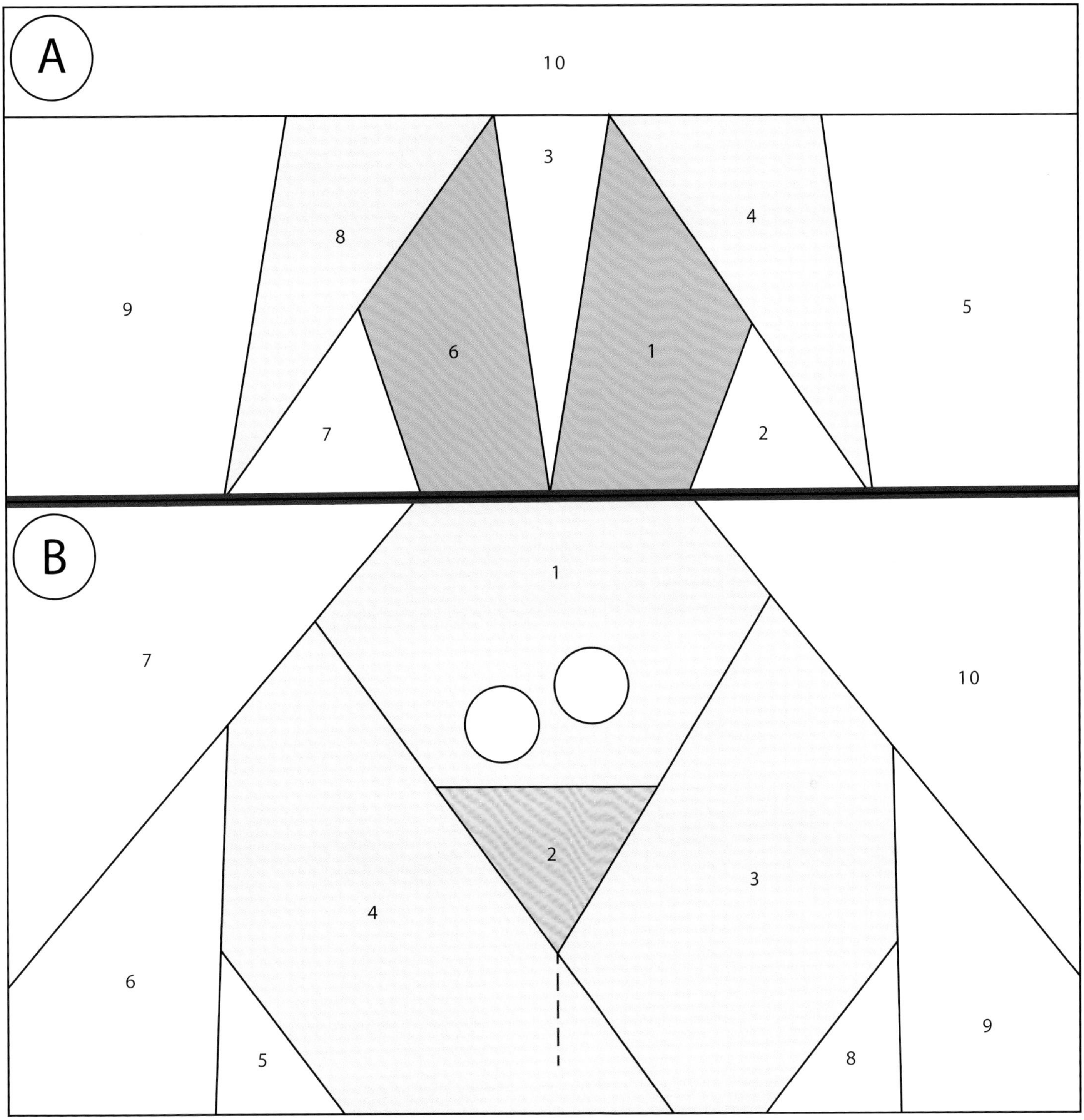

BUNNY

MATERIALS

- Large scrap of white, at least 9″ × 11″
- Scraps of light blue, medium blue, and pink
- 2 white ½″ buttons and 2 black ⅛″ buttons for eyes
- Black embroidery floss

DIRECTIONS

For detailed directions, refer to Paper-Piecing Basics (page 7).

1. Make 2 copies of the pattern (A, B).
2. Cut around each segment, adding ¼″ seam allowances.
3. Paper piece each segment.
4. Connect the segments: A to B.
5. Embroider the mouth with the paper still attached.
6. Trim the block to 8″ × 8″.

When directed in the project instructions, remove the paper from the back of the block and hand sew any buttons on.

Elliot

ABOUT THE AUTHOR

Mary (also known as Marney) Hertel grew up on a small dairy farm in the heart of Wisconsin. Sewing is in her blood, and she likes to say she has "sewn since birth," starting on her mother's sewing machine at a very early age. She was drawn to sewing like a moth to a flame, and after securing her art education job straight out of college, she used her first paycheck to purchase a sewing machine. Soon after, she started to quilt and has never stopped.

Mary's favorite method of quilting became paper piecing after she was introduced to this practice in 2013. The puzzle-like quality of paper piecing appealed to Mary and has quickly become her favorite approach to adding an image to a quilt.

Her quirky animal designs are a nod to 35 years of teaching children's art. "I try to keep my animal designs childlike, but expressive," Mary says. She also strives to offer her customers very easy paper-pieced patterns.

Enjoy her whimsical designs and her easy-to-paper-piece patterns.

Also by Mary Hertel:

Visit Mary online and follow on social media:

Website: madebymarney.com

Facebook: /madebymarney

Pinterest: /maryhertel

Instagram: @madebymarney

Twitter: @madebymarney

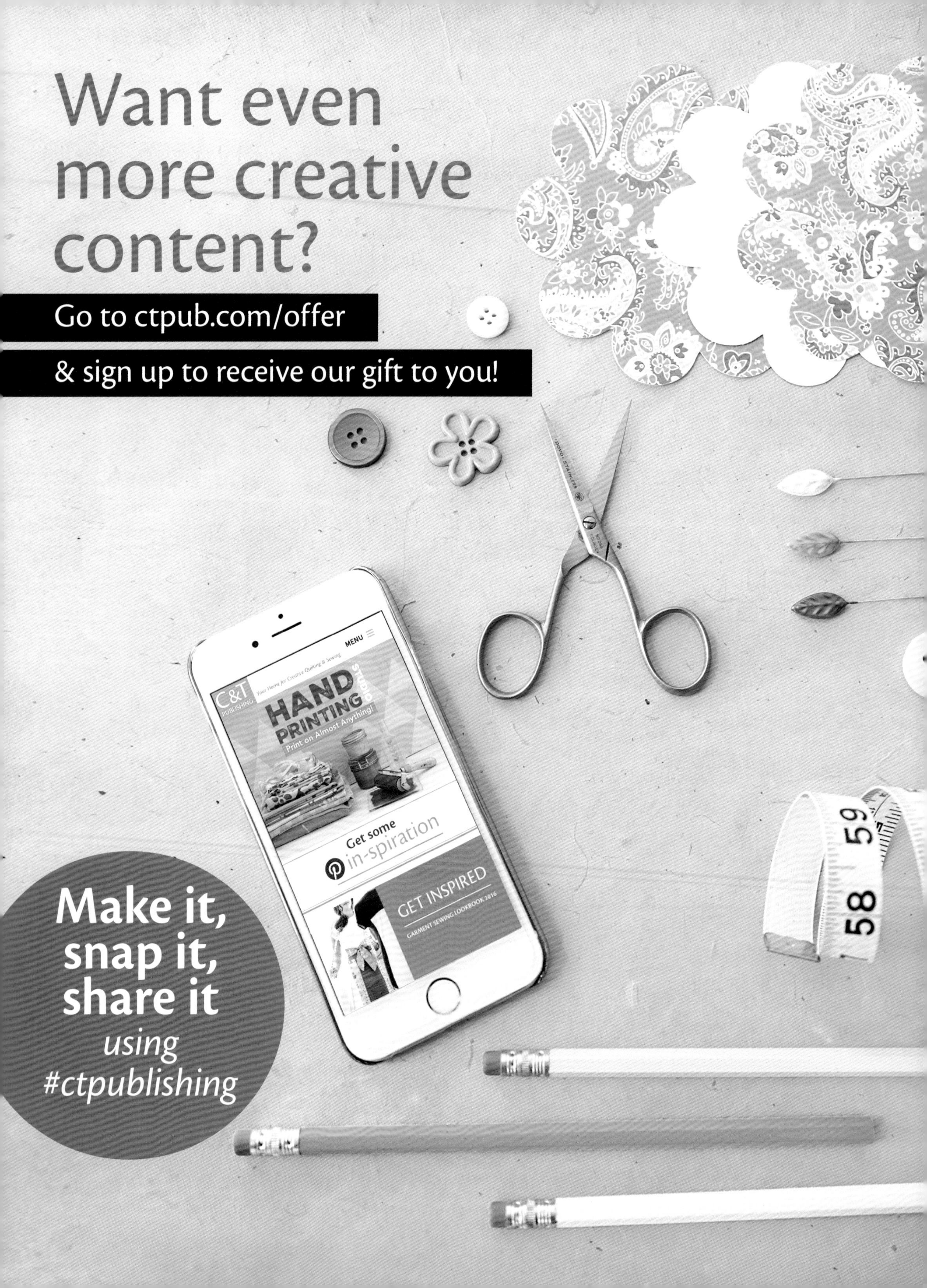
Want even more creative content?
Go to ctpub.com/offer
& sign up to receive our gift to you!
MENU
C&T PUBLISHING
Your Home for Creative Quilting & Sewing
HAND PRINTING STUDIO
Print on Almost Anything!
Get some in-spiration
GET INSPIRED
GARMENT SEWING LOOKBOOK 2016
Make it, snap it, share it using #ctpublishing